Leadership
in the
Reagan
Presidency

Leadership
in the
Reagan Presidency

Seven Intimate Perspectives

Paul Laxalt
Tom Griscom
Donald Thomas Regan
Lyn Nofziger
Fred Barnes
Lou Cannon
Sander Vanocur

Edited by
Kenneth W. Thompson

MADISON BOOKS
Lanham • New York • London

Co-published by arrangement with The Miller Center
of Public Affairs, University of Virginia.

Published by Madison Books
4720 Boston Way
Lanham, Maryland 20706

Distributed by National Book Network

The views expressed by the author(s) of this publication
do not necessarily represent the opinions of the Miller
Center. We hold to Jefferson's dictum that: "Truth is the
proper and sufficient antagonist to error, and has
nothing to fear from the conflict, unless by human
interposition, disarmed of her natural weapons, free
argument and debate."

The paper used in this publication meets the minimum
requirements of American National Standard for
Information Sciences—Permanence of Paper for
Printed Library Materials, ANSI Z39.48–1984. ∞™
Manufactured in the United States of America.

Library of Congress Cataloging-in-Publication Data

The Reagan Presidency : Seven Intimate Perspectives / edited by Kenneth W. Thompson.
    p.   cm. — (Portraits of American Presidents ; v. 9)
Contents: pt. 1. Leadership.
1. United States—Politics and government—1981–
1989.   2. Reagan, Ronald.   I. Thompson, Kenneth
W., 1921–   .   II. Series.
E176.1.P83   1982 vol. 9
[E876]
973.927'092—dc20   91–33844 CIP

ISBN 0–8191–8473–X (cloth : alk. paper)
ISBN 0–8191–8474–8 (pbk. : alk. paper)

With grateful thanks

to participants

in the Reagan Oral History

CONTENTS

CONTENTS

II. REAGAN AS LEADER:
VIEWS FROM OUTSIDERS

PREFACE

One sign of the contemporaneity of the Reagan administration is the projected publication of four or five volumes on the Reagan presidency by the Miller Center. In approaching the Reagan oral history, we have reaped the benefits of participation by a larger number of witnesses and subjects than with any previous postwar presidency. With the Miller Center's Roosevelt oral history, no more than a half dozen high-ranking officials from that administration were available. With the greater availability of the Reagan official family, we have already exceeded 50 participants.

On the other side of this advantage, we lack the authoritative historical sources, the monographs, and scholarly articles and the reconsiderations or revisions that enrich the study of earlier presidencies. No point is served in discounting the benefits of historical perspective. Such perspective is clearly lacking in the search for truth in the 1980s. With the Reagan presidency, if not all postwar presidencies, we approach a historical era the end of which is not yet in sight. We are dealing with a story viewed only from its beginning, its midpoint, and a few high points. At best we have only the most fragmentary knowledge of the consequences. Our task is the more complex because of the ideological divisions surrounding the Reagan presidency. Within and outside the administration, historians and scholars as well as policymakers cluster together around different value systems.

However, the limits of sources and possible observer bias are nothing new in the annals of political history. James Madison wrote of such limits, saying:

It has been a misfortune of history that a *personal knowledge* and an *impartial judgment* of things can *rarely meet* in the historian. The best history of our country therefore must be the fruit of contributions bequeathed by co-temporary actors and witnesses, to successors who will make an unbiased use of them.

But Madison took heart from the fact that future historians and scholars might find in such early histories the sources on which more detached and objective studies could be written. His optimism about historical interpretation is one we share. It lies at the center of our commitment to oral histories. We make bold to suggest that future historians of the Reagan administration will draw on these early findings. The participants in the inquiry have helped lay foundations for future research.

Madison concluded:

And if the abundance and authenticity of the materials . . . should descend to hands capable of doing justice to them, then American history can be expected to contain more truth, and *lessons . . . not less valuable*, than that of *any country or age* whatever [italics added].

INTRODUCTION

We have chosen as the framework for Part I on leadership in the Reagan presidential portrait series a division among insiders and outsiders to the administration. The insiders include a senator from Nevada who was perhaps Reagan's most trusted friend. They also include a communications expert, a Wall Street executive who served both as secretary of the treasury and chief of staff, and a political adviser from Reagan's days as governor of California and through his campaigns for the presidency.

The outsiders include a Reagan partisan who writes for *The New Republic*, a biographer and columnist who covered Reagan in California and Washington, and a prominent television commentator.

Our purpose is to draw on a broadly representative group of interpreters whose histories shed light on different facets of the Reagan administration. Those who follow in subsequent volumes will contribute new perspectives not as evident in this first volume. Some will be critics who are more outspoken than any in this volume. Others quite possibly will propose views of the Reagan presidency even more supportive of the administration than any in this collection. In this way the multiple volumes in the series will have a progressive and unfolding character, each adding to what has gone before in the accounts of the Reagan presidency.

Appropriately, Senator Paul Laxalt of Nevada is the author of the first chapter. His oral history constitutes the personal reflections of a seasoned political friend. Throughout his political career, Ronald Reagan has turned repeatedly to Paul Laxalt for advice and counsel. They were fellow governors in California and Nevada. Laxalt was Reagan's confidant in the Senate. The senator confesses that at first, especially in the mid-1970s, he questioned whether Reagan was in the presidential league. The more he saw the so-called big leaguers, however, the better Reagan looked. None of the others had the charisma, popular appeal, and conviction that Reagan had.

Laxalt sees Reagan as the citizen-politician. He demonstrates that such a candidate can win if properly handled. Like Theodore Roosevelt, he used "the bully pulpit" to go over the heads of the Congress when they opposed him. He had a few simple principles which he believed and applied with remarkable consistency.

1.   The federal government is too big. Power should shift to the states;

2.   People are overtaxed and deserve tax cuts; and

3.   It may be possible to deal with the Soviets from strength. Hence, he fought to build up the national defense.

While personal throughout, Laxalt offers an overview of Reagan that presents his strengths but hints that he had some weaknesses: Reagan may have been wrong on the deficit and on those policies that led to its creation.

Tom Griscom is the extremely able former assistant and press secretary to Senator Baker who accompanied Baker when he became chief of staff in the Reagan administration. He served as assistant to the President for communication and planning. He was principally involved in planning and coordinating two summit conferences and in particular masterminding the Reagan speeches at the Moscow summit. Griscom restates, in terms somewhat different from Laxalt's, the Reagan mandate as the President saw it.

Griscom made the thought-provoking suggestion that Reagan, having lived by the media in the communicating of his policy goals, was more vulnerable than other presidents might have been when Iran-contra occurred. (He who lives by the media . . .) He also supports the view that Reagan made social programs such as abortion and prayer in the schools subordinate to his economic goals when he came to office. Even more than Laxalt, Griscom while praising Reagan goes on to show that, on issues such as Social Security, he, like others, failed. Griscom attributes a policy axiom to Reagan: "Go for a program if you believe in it, but don't lose sight of where the public stands. If the issue is too divisive, you will lose more than its worth." Such an axiom brings to light Reagan's pragmatic nature. The second half of his testimony deals with the last two years of the Reagan presidency.

As most readers of books on the presidency as well as the public at large know, Donald Regan is the author of a controversial book on the Reagan presidency. In his oral history, he goes beyond the book and says little or nothing about Nancy Reagan's astrologer. He defends the deficit as being less important than many believe. He paints a more favorable picture of Reagan than reviewers of his earlier book led us to expect. He makes the argument that Reagan was a politician willing to compromise on most issues, whereas some chief executives in business expect that their decisions once made are commands which are beyond compromise or interpretation. Regan compares cash and capital budgets and uses the comparison to minimize the impact of the deficit. He also comments at length on his role as chief of staff.

Lyn Nofziger's history is an intensely personal political profile of Ronald Reagan. More perhaps even than Laxalt, he talks about Reagan as a person, having known him over the span of his entire political career. He provides fresh vignettes of Reagan, such as his reservations about flying during the years from 1945 to 1965. He emphasizes Reagan's sense of timing, for example, in announcing he was going to run for governor and later for president. He discusses Reagan's feelings when he lost as well as when he won and his sense that in 1968 he was not ready to be president.

Nofziger shows that Reagan did not take himself or his work as seriously as many governors and presidents have done. He tells a hilarious story of Reagan's lecturing his staff about going home to their wives and families rather than working late on matters that were not all that important. Nofziger offers unique insights on Reagan's approach to difficult decisions, for example, involving capital punishment. He discusses Reagan's divorce from Jane Wyman and his determination to make his second marriage succeed. He confirms that there will always be a veil between Ronald Reagan and the rest of the world, whether to protect himself from being hurt or because he had been a movie actor harried by people who wanted his favors: as "private as a Trappist monk." Throughout his oral history, Nofziger opens a window on the personal aspects of Reagan's life and work.

In the second half of the book, three columnists and commentators offer some outsiders' views of Reagan. Fred Barnes of *The New Republic* is conspicuously a Reagan partisan. He introduces his history by noting that Reagan is a passive person who had a very active presidency, comparing him in this respect to President Bush. (It should be noted that he did his oral history prior to the Gulf War.) He speaks of Reagan's reading habits and his dependence on conservative publications such as *Human Events*. In explaining why he had not aged, Reagan told the story of the old and the young psychiatrist. The latter was weary at the end of a long day of counseling, the former was happy and upbeat. When asked why, the latter replied, "I don't listen."

Barnes finds Reagan's first term clearly superior to his second, when his policies were eclipsed by the downfall of communism. Barnes speaks of his arms negotiating tactics, his conversion to supply-side economics, and his strategy with SDI. These sections reveal Reagan's predilection for large and sweeping solutions to problems. He closes with a recitation of Reagan jokes. All represent *moments* in Reagan's political career.

Lou Cannon may be the most indefatigable American journalist in covering a single political figure. His beat for the *San Jose Mercury News* and the *Washington Post* has been Ronald Reagan. He wrote one of the early Reagan books centered on the rivalry between Reagan and Jessie Unruh. What is distinctive in his account is its camera stop focus which is set on 1986. At that point, Cannon saw Reagan at the crossroads on issues such as arms negotiations and the deficit. He throws light on Reagan's skill in answering political questions in press conferences despite the apprehension of his press and political advisers. All this is important in understanding Reagan as a communicator and where he stood in the sixth year of his presidency. These are the focal points in Cannon's 1986 oral history. On a lighter note, Cannon reveals how he began and continued his collection of Reaganisms.

Sander Vanocur approaches Ronald Reagan from having been an admirer of John F. Kennedy and Hubert Humphrey. Thus his discussion of the Reagan legacy is less that of a partisan and more that of someone whose more favorable view of Reagan has evolved over time. He doubts there is a Reagan legacy if by that one means significant political realignment. He judges Reaganomics to have been a failure, reflected most notably in the deficit. However, he credits such successes as the country's prosperity to Reagan's proclivity to treat "reality as an illusion that must be overcome."

Vanocur analyzes Reagan's successes from the standpoint of the political groups and parties with whom he worked. In doing so he goes back to Wendell Willkie to trace change and continuity in the composition of the Republican party. He introduces the idea of "middle-class populism" as a factor in Reagan's political following. More than any other participant in the Reagan oral history thus far, Vanocur seeks to understand Reagan in relationship to underlying forces in American politics. In the end, however, he concludes that his achievements are in large part due to certain personal characteristics, such as a complete lack of political or personal rancor.

Taken together, the seven histories set us on the trail of a far better understanding of Ronald Reagan and the Reagan presidency.

I

REAGAN AS LEADER:

PERSPECTIVES FROM INSIDERS

CHAPTER 1

REAGAN: PERSONAL REFLECTIONS OF A FRIEND

PAUL LAXALT

NARRATOR: During our discussions of the Reagan administration, one name has continued to be mentioned. Repeatedly we have been told that the one person we should ask to participate in our oral history of President Reagan is Senator Paul Laxalt.

Paul Laxalt received both his bachelor's and law degrees from the University of Denver. He has been a district attorney, a city attorney, and both lieutenant governor and governor of Nevada. A fellow governor at one time with Ronald Reagan, he served faithfully and with great dignity in the United States Senate from 1974 to 1986. In addition, he was perhaps Ronald Reagan's closest friend and confidant, as symbolized in the historic trip that he made to the Philippines to discuss the change in government there with Mr. Marcos.

There are many more things one could say—law firms with which he has served and honors which he has received. We count it a high privilege to welcome Senator Laxalt to Mr. Jefferson's academical village.

SENATOR LAXALT: Thank you very kindly, Ken. I guess many things could be said about Ken Thompson. From my own experience I would say he is a study in persistence. We have been attempting to put this together for at least three or four years, and I must say my not having come earlier should not be interpreted as any reluctance to come back to this beautiful place. I've had occasion over the years, particularly when I was in the Senate, to

3

come here and speak to some of your students. Many of them here, as well as many of the people throughout Virginia, constituted the base of the Reagan candidacies, starting back in 1976.

I am certain that people like Howard Baker and Ed Meese have done a good job in presenting the policies of Ronald Reagan as well as the Reagan presidency itself. Therefore, what I would like to do is give you the benefit of my unique perspective in having been very close to Ronald Reagan, both personally and politically, for a long time. I would like to talk about his California days, his 1976 presidential campaign, and the campaigns of 1980 and 1984. I would like to conclude with some general observations about the Reagan presidency, and then answer any questions you might have.

I first became exposed to Ronald Reagan on a personal and political basis in 1964. That was the time of the Goldwater presidential campaign—an exercise in futility in the minds of many people, but not in mine. At the time I was a very young lieutenant governor in Nevada and was the first public official in the West to publicly commit for Barry Goldwater. During the course of that campaign, I spoke at an event in California at which Ronald Reagan spoke as well. In my own mind at that time, Reagan had no public persona. He was a fine man and an actor whose work I enjoyed, but like many people at that time, I believed he was of questionable political substance.

However, it was during the Goldwater campaign that he attracted national attention because of a speech he made in Los Angeles. It was a magnificent speech lasting almost half an hour; it was televised, and was probably the most exciting event during the course of the entire Goldwater campaign. Whether he realized it or not, Reagan had then come to the attention of many prominent political types in California—as well as throughout the country—who insisted in 1965 that he run for governor of California.

He had difficulty with that decision, because although he enjoyed politics, he hadn't really thought in terms of being a candidate. Many of his old actor friends tell me that in their acting days he constantly talked politics. Most of them weren't politically oriented so they considered this constant political interest to be somewhat of a drag and a bore. Nonetheless, Reagan persisted, and in 1966 he decided to run for governor; at the same time I decided to run for governor of Nevada.

We had parallel campaigns, kept track of one another, and were both elected. During the course of our governorships we had many problems in common, since our states adjoined. In particular, we had a huge problem in connection with Lake Tahoe, a magnificent area, which at the time was being overdeveloped. We were fearful of the adverse ecological effects which many ecologists said were probable if this overdevelopment on the lake continued. Consequently, if you can believe it, two staunch conservatives decided that the only way to deal with the problem was for us to create a huge metropolitan agency that would cover both states. We did that, and as a result we prevented the overdevelopment of Tahoe and have preserved it. Both of us are rather proud of that.

During that period of time, Reagan did a lot of exciting things in California that brought him national attention. I would think then, as now, there are very few states that are as complex politically and have as many nagging problems as California. He approached these problems aggressively and, I thought, interestingly, because he approached them as a citizen-politician. He proceeded immediately to slash programs right and left. He incurred the animosity of most of the university structure in California; he wasn't exactly their darling during the 1960s. It wasn't all that safe to go with Ronald Reagan to any California campus. For that matter, it wasn't safe for many of the rest of us either.

However, he continued on that course, particularly on the spending side. He had at that time what many of us feel the President of the United States should have: the line-item veto. I saw him employ that hundreds of times and save the people of California literally billions of dollars. When he became governor of California, the state faced a very difficult fiscal situation; during the course of his governorship and thereafter, the state was actually sending refunds to its citizens. Absolutely remarkable!

After four years as governor of Nevada, I left politics to do other things, but Reagan continued as governor of California and was elected to another four-year term in 1970.

We remained in contact during those years, but we weren't all that close. In 1974 I decided to get back into politics and ran for the United States Senate during the Watergate scandal—a remarkable sense of political timing. Somehow I won, and as you all remember, in 1974 Gerald Ford succeeded to the presidency under the most difficult of circumstances and was doing an admirable job. At that time, many of the Reagan people and many of the conservatives throughout the country felt that while Gerald Ford had been a very effective caretaker president, he probably wouldn't be a strong enough candidate to get reelected. As a result, many people solicited Ronald Reagan for the purpose of considering a run in 1976 for the presidency.

You can imagine the heartburn that created in many circles, because to run against an incumbent sitting president in either party simply isn't done. It's tacky and is politically dangerous if you don't make it. I must say that when I went back to Washington in 1974 I had in mind that, while the Reagan people felt he should run for president—he did have an abortive run in 1968 in Miami which was very amateurish and which didn't go anywhere—he really wasn't in the presidential league. However, I must add that the longer I was in Washington and the more I saw the so-called "big leaguers," the better Ronald Reagan looked to me. I found that for the most part, these big leaguers didn't have the charisma, the appeal, and the conviction that Ronald Reagan had.

At a dinner in 1975 at the Madison Hotel in Washington, there were four or five of us with Ronald Reagan considering whether or not he should look at a presidential run. I often think about that dinner because the Reagan presidency really began that evening. It illustrated to me what could happen in this politically complex and overwhelming country if you can gather a handful of people with enough conviction to even seek the presidency. Reagan decided that he would not commit at that time to run for the presidency. He wanted a feasibility study, which I suppose is a product of his General Electric days, so he commissioned several of us and asked me to lead the study. He wanted to know if a Reagan candidacy would be divisive to the Republican party. He didn't want to get involved in any effort that was going to be unduly divisive, because he believed strongly in the two-party system and had become a very dedicated Republican, particularly as governor of California. We took some samplings around the country and came to the conclusion that if the candidacy were performed in a positive way it need not be divisive. Eventually that report was made to him and he decided to run.

I think the 1976 contest for the Republican nomination between Reagan and Ford was probably one of the most civilized I have ever seen at any level. They are both gentlemen. There were no slashing personal attacks of the type that you see now since negative campaigning and negative advertising have unfortunately become vogue. They both presented to the Republicans of this country their various views of how the presidency should be conducted in the future.

We finally came down to the wire, as before the convention neither side had the requisite number to lock up the nomination and advance the convention. There were about 100 uncommitted delegates floating around who were eventually going to make the difference. I can remember being in competition with President Ford for those delegates, even though it really wasn't a fair competition; President Ford, utilizing the White House, as well he should, was inviting delegates there. He would have them picked up in limousines for visits to the Oval Office and the Roosevelt Room, and for receptions in the East Room as well.

Reagan was losing that battle for these delegates quickly because all we could do was call people and ask them for their vote. Therefore, we came to the conclusion that we needed to do something very exciting, lest the race be locked up. It was finally decided that what Reagan needed, and this was unprecedented, was a vice presidential candidate, preferably someone from the same area as the uncommitted delegates. In that particular year, as in many years, most of these delegates were from larger eastern and northeastern states like New Jersey, Pennsylvania, and New York. We finally decided therefore that we would solicit my seatmate in the United States Senate, Richard Schweiker from Pennsylvania, as a running mate in advance. He was shocked, but flattered, and in one of the more exciting press conferences I have ever seen in my life in the Capitol, it was announced that Richard Schweiker was going to be the vice presidential running mate for Ronald Reagan. Since Richard Schweiker had an image of being somewhat left of center, I think there was some consternation, particularly among my conservative colleagues. In particular, I remember Strom Thurmond saying, "But Paul, Schweiker is a liberal!" We proceeded, however, with that bold move to at least unsettle the situation so that these remaining delegates waited until the convention before they committed.

The Republican national convention of 1976 was by far the most exciting convention that I have ever participated in because it went right down to the wire; we were dead even. Both sides were fighting for every delegate; it was democracy at its best. We took a test vote in which we lost, narrowly, and I'll never forget what Dick Schweiker did the next morning. He said that he had examined the test vote and had come to the conclusion that the reason Ronald Reagan did not prevail was because of him. In particular Dick said that there had been some defections in some of the Southern states like Mississippi, and that he thought it would be better if he withdrew from the ticket to give Ronald Reagan a better chance. Without a moment's hesitation Ronald Reagan said, "No. We came on this together and we are going out together." This was a moment of truth which I thought reflected the character and integrity of both Ronald Reagan and Richard Schweiker. Finally, of course, Gerald Ford was nominated, and all of us pitched in to help him; as you recall, he was narrowly defeated by Jimmy Carter.

At this time Reagan was in his late 60s, and most people believed that at that age a person was no longer viable for any public office, particularly the presidency. I think the Reagans felt that they had had their chance and that was it. I implored them to stay loose because they had made a very positive impression, not only upon Republicans, but upon the country as well. I told them that politics was unpredictable and cyclical and that you never knew what would happen. Even though it is conventional wisdom that if a sitting president does a good job, ordinarily he will have eight years—and eight years would be out of the question for the Reagans—I asked them to stay loose.

I remember attending my first meeting as a senator with President Carter. It was several weeks into his presidency, and it was apparent to me then that as decent a man as he was and as competent as he was in some areas, he just didn't have it; he just didn't relate. He didn't even come close to relating to us as senators, not that that was the test. Therefore, that day after the meeting I called Ronald Reagan and told him that I thought I had just met a one-term president and strongly advised him not to make any public Shermanesque-type statements about not running for the presidency in the future. I thought that, depending upon future developments, the climate would be right so that Ronald Reagan would be a viable candidate in 1980. As you know, eventually he decided to run and conducted a tremendous campaign in 1980.

   We had developed a team of pros in 1976 and kept them on
in 1980. However, some of them weren't tactically up to the 1980
race, especially in Iowa. Ronald Reagan, as many of you know, had
his roots in the Illinois-Iowa area as a young man and spent much
of his youth after graduating from college as a sports announcer in
Des Moines. Therefore, some of our political pros felt that he
didn't have to spend much time in Iowa, and that instead he should
spend his time in other more important states. George Bush was
running then, and he practically lived in Iowa for months. To the
complete shock of the whole political community in this country,
and particularly to the Reagan forces, Bush beat Ronald Reagan in
Iowa. That loss awoke the Reagan forces, and a new strategy and
new people were found so that the campaign could go forward.
   I'll never forget a debate we had at a small school auditorium
in Nashua, New Hampshire. George Bush, Ronald Reagan, and
several other candidates such as Howard Baker and Phil Crane
participated, but the stars were really Bush and Reagan. A
parliamentary struggle developed as to whether Ronald Reagan or
George Bush was to speak first, and the moderator turned off
Ronald Reagan's mike. Because the Reagan forces had essentially
paid for the cost of the whole event, Ronald Reagan grabbed the
mike and said, "Mr. Green, I refuse to be turned off; I paid for the
mike!" It was explosive! It showed a fighting spirit that Ronald
Reagan had never before displayed. Psychologically, I think that
little outburst completely broke the logjam as far as Ronald Reagan
was concerned in New Hampshire and in the rest of the country.
In New Hampshire he won a convincing victory over George Bush.
   It wasn't easy early in the campaign because the people who
had been running it had acted like political sultans. We had $18
million that we could spend on the entire campaign, but after New
Hampshire, we found that we had already spent $12 million.
Therefore, we had $6 million for the rest of the country to cover the
remainder of the campaign, and George Bush was still a very viable
and well-financed candidate.
   In desperation, we went to a fellow by the name of Bill Casey.
I had never known Mr. Casey, but apparently he had power in
financial circles in New York and was well respected as a hardball
man who could watch a dollar. He had also been in the Nixon
administration and was considered to be a good political strategist.
Out of desperation, and at the personal request of the Reagans,

Casey was brought onto the campaign. He didn't really have a public persona, and you couldn't understand a word he said (in fact, when Bill was the head of the CIA we used to tease him by saying that he would never need a scrambler since no one could ever understand anything he said), but in my estimation he did a magnificent job.

He grabbed hold of that campaign, watched and nursed every nickel, used a minimum amount of television advertising, and I bet you that if you could somehow measure the expeditious use of presidential campaign money, nothing would have ever matched that campaign. We went through the whole rest of that campaign without wasting any money; we cut our work force, relied on volunteers—which is not in vogue anymore—and proceeded to have a wonderful race, an unprecedented landslide. On the evening of the election at about 5 o'clock California time, the Reagans were preparing to go to dinner with some friends when Jimmy Carter called and conceded.

In 1984 he ran against Mr. Mondale, with whom I served in the Senate—a magnificent man. He represented, however, an ideology which was not acceptable at the time to most Americans. Despite this, and despite the fact that Reagan seemingly had everything going for him (he was an incumbent President, had a strong political organization, and was at least on a par with Mr. Mondale in the fund-raising area), he almost fumbled the campaign in one of the worst events that I have ever seen politically: the Reagan-Mondale debate in Kentucky. The debate was a total, unmitigated disaster. Ronald Reagan stumbled through it, he wasn't responsive, and his closing statement was abysmal. This could have immediately been very destructive because a lot of people thought that while he was a wonderful man, he'd had four years and was now over the hill. Reagan's poor performance during this debate seemed proof positive of this belief.

Many of us examined what had happened and came to the conclusion that Ronald Reagan had been overtrained for the debate. He had been put into too many mock debates with people like David Stockman who would play Mondale and would be all over him and in his face, as the kids now say. Reagan's people loaded his head with numbers to the point that when he went into Kentucky he had a psychological straitjacket on him and performed miserably. Therefore, we decided that the second debate would be played differently; we didn't get into many debating sessions at all, but instead simply discussed issues in a general way, without stuffing any statistics into the President's head. The results of the second debate were quite different, as once again the old Ronald Reagan emerged and performed magnificently, and all that had been lost was retrieved.

Near the end of the campaign, when it was apparent that Ronald Reagan was going to win and win easily—every poll revealed that—we were flying over the upper Midwest, and several of Mr. Reagan's aides said they had received responses from Minnesota asking him to make a visit. To show what kind of gentleman he is, Ronald Reagan replied, "I don't really want to go into Minnesota because that's Mr. Mondale's home area and I'd rather not go in there at all." I'll never forget that, because this is after Fritz had already visited California, and with no trepidation whatsoever. However, on the weekend before the election, people in Minnesota were absolutely demanding that Reagan make a stop in their state, however briefly, so we threw together a brief airport appearance. One hour before we landed we put the word out through the radio that Ronald Reagan was going to come to this isolated rural airport, and as we flew in, I couldn't believe what I saw. There were trucks and automobiles coming in from every road from miles around, and on one hour's notice, 10,000 people had come to greet Ronald Reagan. He made a very gracious speech in Minnesota, and as you know, Minnesota was the only state that Ronald Reagan didn't carry—a very convincing victory to say the least.

I will leave the evaluations of the Reagan presidency for the historians because my views are somewhat biased. However, I think certain observations can be made. First, any citizen-politician, if properly handled and if in possession of the qualities necessary to become a candidate—even in these modern and sophisticated days—can realistically aspire to be elected President of the United States. That makes me as a citizen feel somewhat reassured, because from the beginning, Ronald Reagan was not a politician—not that I consider that to be bad—but he was basically a citizen who got into politics on a short-term, temporary basis. He also demonstrated that the power of the presidency, in terms of its being a "bully pulpit" as Teddy Roosevelt used to say, was absolutely awesome if properly utilized.

Having been inside the Reagan presidency, I was impressed by how limited a president is as a political force, because the plain truth is that the real power is in the administrative areas. It's almost irrelevant who the President of the United States is because the career bureaucrats run it. They see presidents come and go, and they do their thing regardless of who the president is and what philosophy he holds. By and large, that's not bad, because most of the people in the administrative areas are very qualified and dedicated.

However, in the areas where you really have to energize the country in dealing with Congress—the policy areas—the presidency can be an enormously effective bully pulpit, and this was Reagan's strength. I can remember in the old days that the Congress wasn't as recalcitrant as it is now. In the post-Watergate era, members of Congress are a new breed; they don't do something simply because the president wants them to do it, or because the leadership in Congress wants them to do it. They are motivated more by fear than by persuasion. Therefore, while Reagan very often couldn't convince the Congress of his position on major policy issues, the members knew that they had better not cross him because he would get on television and appeal to their constituencies and build up enormous constituent pressure. The mail and telephone calls that he was able to engender through his public appearances were absolutely awesome. On issue after issue I saw him change the complexion of Congress on key votes because he had that capability. Admittedly, toward the end of his presidency, that power diminished because of the Iran-contra situation; he did lose influence over the Congress after that. Overall, however, he did demonstrate how effective a president can be.

Lastly, I think that whatever you may say about Reagan or his record, and however you may feel philosophically, he had a basic adherence to several simple principles. First, he felt that the federal government was too big and too expensive. He believed that the size of the federal government, if it couldn't effectively be reduced, should at least be restrained to permit state and local governments to grow more. Second, he felt that the people are overtaxed and that we should have tax cuts, which would stimulate the economy and promote economic growth. Third, and most importantly, he felt that we were in a tenuous place in respect to the Soviets, and that the only way to deal effectively with them was to build an effective defense force. Reagan was convinced that if we did that, particularly with something like SDI, the Soviets would come to the negotiating table.

History will probably indicate that his basic principles at the time were valid and that he was effective enough to be able to carry them out. In addition, there are many who feel that with the events of the last several months, Ronald Reagan hasn't been given due credit for what has happened in Eastern Europe and in the Soviet Union. That may or may not be true, but as far as he is concerned, it's not a problem for him; he's basically an unselfish man. I visited with him recently in Los Angeles. He had just returned from a trip to Eastern Europe and Berlin, and I think he knows that the people there recognize and appreciate what he has done for them.

His staff tells me that in Berlin, and wherever he went in the Soviet Union, the people absolutely lionized him and gave him substantial credit for the fact that they had been liberated. They so indicated to him, and I have never seen him as appreciative of his efforts in public life as he is now. For an old friend and associate like me, that's reassuring, because very often politics doesn't turn out that way.

QUESTION: You spoke a few times about Mr. Reagan's age. Could you tell us what changes you have observed during your 25 years of acquaintance with Mr. Reagan in his memory, level of energy, and capacity for sustaining concentration and activity? If there have been changes, did they affect his ability to function as the chief executive?

SENATOR LAXALT: In terms of his physical energy and in terms of his alertness, I don't know that there has been any fundamental change. He is one of the few people I know who is virtually ageless. He does suffer from a hearing problem, which I think at times serves him well. There were times during debates or discussions in which he wasn't particularly interested when he would start to turn off and I knew what had happened. Essentially, Ronald Reagan was a delegator, so he didn't have to be a nitty-gritty type of person. During the time that we were governors together, I was absolutely amazed at how much he delegated out. I couldn't do that! I had to know what was going on in my shop. I don't know whether I was nosy or curious or if I just didn't have that degree of confidence.

Thus, it wasn't required for him in terms of administration to have the degree of alertness that one normally would, although I'm sure that he did.

The same thing happened in the White House. He delegated almost everything out and never looked back, and for the most part it served him well. It blew up on him in the Iran-contra affair, because he didn't know what was going on in the basement, and he should have. In the last days in the Iran-contra period, I sensed that he was hurt because he received criticism from the people. He always had received it from certain quarters of the press, but to receive it from the people, who in poll after poll indicated that they didn't believe him, hurt him to the core.

As I said, however, I haven't seen any real change in him in terms of his energy. He is really energetic, even now. He was 80 years old in February 1991, and he is still positive, alert, and above all, I think, passive and serene; what a joy it must be after all the tumultuous years to be 80 years old and be at peace. He's actually always been at peace, because he has always been kind and gentle.

In the raucous and difficult world of Washington politics, I can remember many times when people really close to the President very often appeared to betray him. Yet, he was always able to look at the positive side of those situations and always able to give those people the benefit of the doubt. For example, when David Stockman went to the press to express his disagreement with Reagan's economic policies, there were many people close to the President, including myself, who felt that Dave should go: not into the woodshed, but into oblivion. You can't tolerate that kind of behavior at that level, and yet Reagan still had a kind word for David. That demonstrates, I think, one of the more subtle qualities that made Ronald Reagan one of our most popular presidents.

QUESTION: It has been suggested by some that the Strategic Defense Initiative was the most important factor in convincing the Soviets to come back to the bargaining table. Do you think that this is an overstatement?

SENATOR LAXALT: No, I don't. I agree with it completely. I'm personally convinced that the Soviets would have never come back to the table in Geneva if it hadn't been clear that Reagan was going forward aggressively with SDI. I don't think you can overexaggerate the importance and the effect that SDI had in the geopolitical and strategic considerations of the Soviet Union. If there was a crowning point in the Reagan presidency in terms of security, it was probably SDI.

I'll never forget the first speech that he made in connection with SDI. He was criticized by the press and even within the Congress, and his SDI proposal was dubbed "Star Wars." Yet the people around him felt that SDI would demonstrate not only to the Soviets but also to Third World dictators that we were going to build our own protective defense against possible nuclear attacks. I would hope—even though the record of the Congress these last few days hasn't been all that reassuring—that on some kind of priority basis we continue to do what we can with SDI. Even though the Soviet threat is substantially diminished, I believe that in the years to come the greatest threat that we will face will be from nuclear proliferation in the Third World: for example, the possibility that men like Saddam Hussein may acquire a nuclear capability. We just can't leave ourselves vulnerable to those kinds of developments.

QUESTION: What is your opinion of the current procedure for nominating the vice president? Is it effective?

SENATOR LAXALT: I think that it's all right. While a case could be made that the election of the vice president should be separate from the election of the president—as is the case for lieutenant governors in many states—it seems that what is most important is that the vice president is someone whom the president feels is going to replace him well in the event that the unmentionable should happen. Also, the vice president should be someone in whom the president can have complete trust and confidence in terms of security and very confidential matters. If you throw the process open—which is appealing from a democratic standpoint—so that you have someone who is elected independently by the people, it could cause difficulties. You could end up having a team that would be basically incompatible, both personally and perhaps politically, and I don't think that would be good.

I would like to say something regarding the present situation. Danny Quayle is a friend and was one of my political protégés when I was still in the Senate. I remember well having dinner with

Dan in New Orleans on the night before George Bush made his vice presidential selection. At that time, Dan was among those being mentioned. He approached me and said that he had heard that there was a possibility that he could get the nomination. Then he said, "Do you think I've got a shot?" I said, "Dan, no way!" In fairness to Dan, however, the manner in which that was handled really hurt him grievously from the very beginning.

The first impression that you make in this country—particularly on television—is critical, and once that impression is created it is almost impossible to correct it. Look at what happened with the Quayle situation. The Quayles weren't notified and they weren't conditioned. After he had been selected they had to find Danny and Marilyn, and within minutes he had been thrust into the national spotlight. I'm sure many of you remember his first television appearance after he had been selected. He was so cheerful and so enthusiastic that he looked like a cheerleader. I don't think it was fair to him at all. George simply was pandering to the press by trying to keep some suspense in the convention where you didn't have to. I think Danny should have been told the first of the week. He should have been conditioned and primed so that he wasn't sent up there as a cold candidate. I think probably that was not fair to him, and I think it has been a very important factor in determining why he has had the difficulties that he has had in this country. I proceed on a premise that he is basically competent, which I believe him to be.

QUESTION: As you know, the governor of Nevada and the governors in 42 other states have the line-item veto privilege. Do you believe that such a privilege will ever be given to the President of the United States?

SENATOR LAXALT: No, I really don't. I wish I could tell you that I thought so. The ironic thing about it is that the line-item veto was not harpooned by the Democrats, but instead by the Republicans in the United States Senate. The leading Republican opponent was not only a respected United States senator but also a former governor who in his state had the line-item veto and who exercised it many times: Mark Hatfield. Mark led the fight against it and did so very effectively. His position was that it's a lot different giving the right of the line-item veto to a governor of a state as opposed to the president. He said he would be perfectly comfortable giving that power and authority to Ronald Reagan because he didn't think that he would abuse it. He said, however, that he could think of presidents in recent memory whom he wouldn't want to have that power. One point Mark made was that with the line-item veto the president would have the ability to almost blackmail senators on legislation by threatening to veto their favorite spending projects in return for their support.

His argument convinced many of the undecided senators that as appealing as the line-item veto is, and regardless of how well it works in some states, perhaps it's a little dangerous on the federal level.

QUESTION: The media has begun increasingly to engage in instant analysis immediately after a campaign speech or a political debate. What is your opinion of this practice?

SENATOR LAXALT: I'm not a real fan of political people in television because I find most of them to be totally devoid of any substance, too often focusing on the sensational in how they cover and analyze an event. However, I don't know what you can do about it. They are a fact of life. I like to think that thoughtful people still basically control the process, and thoughtful people are not going to be swayed by "experts" who dissect a State of the Union speech in 30 seconds. I would also hope that thoughtful people are going to be reading periodicals and newspapers and engaging in discussions among themselves.

That was the case in the Reagan effort. The people who influenced policy in his administration were thoughtful people. For example, Jeane Kirkpatrick came from a campus and not from the television. It was because of her writing that she came to the attention of President Reagan and became a forceful factor in the administration. I think that most presidents recognize the distinction between entertainment and substance. Television gives you entertainment but not much substance, and most presidents, when making basic policy decisions, are going to be more substantive in their approach for advice. At least I hope so.

QUESTION: Why did Reagan agree to debate Mondale in 1984 when, as you indicated, it was obvious that Mondale had very little chance of winning the election?

SENATOR LAXALT: Many in the campaign felt that Reagan shouldn't debate Mondale because it would give Mondale additional media coverage. Ronald Reagan, however, believes in public discourse, and it was his decision to go ahead and have the debate.

There were also the so-called political "experts" in the campaign who had no faith in Ronald Reagan's ability to debate. They were afraid to let him out on his own, and they were afraid to let Reagan be Reagan. I used to fight with them over this because in debates and forums of this type, style is far more important than substance; and no one can beat Ronald Reagan on style. Even in the substantive areas, he constantly surprised us. The experts also had no faith in Reagan because they didn't consider him a professional politician, which is one of his greatest strengths.

We were in North Carolina in 1976 after Reagan had been defeated by Gerald Ford in New Hampshire. He blew that race because again, on the advice of political experts, he was told he had New Hampshire in his pocket. Therefore, the weekend before the primary Reagan left New Hampshire and went to Illinois because that's where all the votes were. He lost in New Hampshire by less than a thousand votes, lost in Illinois, and then lost in Florida. So in North Carolina it was do-or-die. One of the great conflicts we had within the campaign was whether or not Ronald Reagan should take advantage of his once being a film actor. The experts (I won't give you names, but you can guess who they were at the time—some inherited from the old Nixon effort) literally wanted to apologize constantly for the fact that Ronald Reagan had at one time been a film actor. They felt somehow that detracted from the seriousness that a presidential candidate should have. They prevailed until North Carolina. We were desperate to find something that worked.

Finally, we brought out a team of his old buddies, and immediately after Jimmy Stewart and the Hollywood crowd came on the scene of the Reagan campaign, the chemistry of the campaign changed. They added a dimension that otherwise you couldn't have had. What the political experts didn't recognize is that politicians per se and political events are dull, unless you are a political junkie. Starting in North Carolina and moving elsewhere, as soon as the Reagan friends were brought in from the film colony, it was unbelievable. As the campaign progressed in the Midwest, our events would draw 2,000 to 3,000 people in areas where normally you would have a few hundred and be happy to have them. This is proof positive that political professionals tend to be very myopic when it comes to seeing the total picture in determining the value of a candidate.

QUESTION: There is some concern about the budget deficits that Ronald Reagan bequeathed us. Did he ever recognize the magnitude of these deficits, and if so did he have any policy initiatives to counter them?

SENATOR LAXALT: If you asked him that question he would say that if the Congress had followed his budget recommendations, the budget would be in balance now; this is open to some questions, because others would say that if you took the Reagan budgets as submitted, we would still have huge deficit problems.

He honestly believed in supply-side economics. He believed that it was necessary to prevent the politicians in Washington from wasting more money, and that if you did that it freed more money for the private sector, and that would regenerate the economy. The fact that we have had the most historic run of economic growth in our history might be proof of that. However, the fact that we have these huge deficits presents the biggest problem in the whole Reagan era, because we honestly felt that if we could exercise restraint on the spending side and combine this with tax incentives to raise revenues, all the ships would rise and all would be well. It simply didn't turn out that way. Our first problem is that we spent more on defense than anyone ever anticipated; defense costs burgeoned literally out of sight. Our second problem is that we were never able, for political reasons, to get the kind of cuts out of the Congress that we should have. I'm convinced that unless we get into a horrid depression, where everybody must really think in terms of sacrifice—particularly in the huge entitlement areas—we will never get the necessary budget cuts from the Congress; the political price is just too great.

The bulk of the spending that we have in this country now is in the so-called entitlement areas. This is where all of the big money items are, and they now account for 70 or 75 percent of government spending. For political reasons, everybody is afraid to touch them. The Congress has tried to realize some savings in the Medicare program before, but because of political pressures they have only been able to achieve modest results. Social Security is the biggest political graveyard in the history of this country. Fooling with Social Security will get you defeated faster than anything else. If you don't believe me, just ask a lot of Republicans who lost in 1982. Unless we get some kind of dictatorial form of government, or if we just get into a total fiscal morass of 1930 proportions, I don't see how we are going to bring this thing into some semblance of balance. I'm afraid it's not going to happen.

I'll never forget when I returned to Washington as a naive young senator in 1974. I had been a balanced-budget governor—a constitutional responsibility—and had campaigned on the basis that we ought to be fiscally conservative. The very first budget that Gerald Ford submitted had a deficit of $23 billion, and I almost went into cardiac arrest! If we could only go back to those glorious days.

Coming back to the Senate chamber one day, I ran into Hubert Humphrey, whom I loved. Hubert Humphrey was a real political scholar and an honest liberal—right or wrong. I asked him about this budget deficit, and he told me not to get excited about things like that, and not to worry about balanced budgets. He said, "A lot of that money we owe to ourselves, anyhow. The real number to keep in your head always is what our debt is in relation to the gross national product." As a young, naive senator, I said, "You know I have all the respect in the world for you, Mr. Humphrey, but every instinct I have tells me that you're wrong." I still believe that, and yet today what are you hearing? You hear that these deficits really don't mean all that much. I have heard several times recently during the budget debate that what is important is what the relation of our deficit is to our GNP, just like Hubert Humphrey told me. I don't know what the answer is.

QUESTION: After Gerald Ford got the Republican nomination in 1976, why didn't Ronald Reagan endorse him?

SENATOR LAXALT: I am asked that question very often, but it's my distinct recollection that Ronald Reagan not only endorsed Gerald Ford, but also campaigned for him extensively. I know because I was on some of those trips with him. Unfortunately, there is this impression that Ronald Reagan backed away from Gerald Ford in that race, and it is simply not true.

NARRATOR: We knew that this discussion was going to be inspiring, but we did not realize just how inspiring it would be. We are very grateful, senator, and we hope you will return to Mr. Jefferson's university soon.

CHAPTER 2

CORE IDEAS
OF THE REAGAN PRESIDENCY

TOM GRISCOM

NARRATOR: Tom Griscom's love of politics began early. He was active in his University of Tennessee at Chattanooga days as a writer on politics. He covered the State Legislature for the News-Free Press of Chattanooga, earning various distinctions. For example, the state legislature introduced a resolution to make him the "State Insect" because he had shown such interest in insects. They also thought of naming the Round House or the university arena after him for the efforts he had made in its behalf. He was active in a host of areas. In the Reagan administration, he has been assistant to the President for communication and planning; he planned both the Washington and the Moscow summits for President Reagan. He also organized, coordinated, and edited those memorable speeches that President Reagan gave in the Soviet Union at the time of the Moscow summit. He is now West Professor of Communication and Public Affairs at the place where the idea of the Miller Center had its birth, namely, Chattanooga, Tennessee. We look forward to years of fruitful relationship between the University of Tennessee at Chattanooga and the work at the Miller Center.

TOM GRISCOM: I thought I would begin by reading two excerpts because I want to focus on how the President was able to use events to set the tone and to manage the things that he did. Primarily, I will look at the last two years when we were at the White House and what we faced when we got there.

First, in this morning's *Wall Street Journal*, Al Hunt, the bureau chief in Washington, refers to the 1988 campaign and its failure to really lay out a mandate. He writes:

> Mr. Reagan used symbols effectively and attacked his opponent, but unlike Mr. Bush, he also laid out the groundwork for governing. The 1980 victory didn't simply reflect discontent with the Democrats. President Carter started off that year ahead of all his potential GOP rivals, but on issues ranging from tax cuts to curbing government regulations and building up America's defenses, Ronald Reagan set an agenda that provided the framework for the successful first Reagan term.

Then he goes on and says: "Ronald Reagan was able to wave a public mandate at Congress—tax cuts, spending cutbacks, and a much tougher defense posture."

The second thing I want to start with is an excerpt from David Broder's book *Behind the Front Page*. In the chapter "Reagan's Way and a Better Way," he says:

> Ronald Reagan's relationship with the press evolved through almost six years of stunningly successful news management, followed by one of the most embarrassing and politically costly blowups in the modern presidency. In only a few weeks a man who seemed a master of presidential public relations saw this image begin to crumble, and this cast into doubt Reagan's political effectiveness in his final two years as President.

I think those are two appropriate points to make as we start out: one, that going into office this President had a mandate for things he wanted to accomplish; and two, that he was very effective in dealing not only with the setting of policy goals, but also in communicating those goals and turning them into actual practice. In doing that, though, he necessarily became a media player and subject to the media's role of interpreting and letting the majority of the people in the country understand what a president is trying to accomplish. Living in that world of the press, then, President Reagan's fate did become somewhat controlled by the press, and this has an effect on being able to continue as an effective leader.

Let's start with 1981. The President came in with a clear set of goals that he wanted to accomplish, and he laid them out in his inaugural address in 1981 on the west front of the Capitol. He talked about cutting the size of government, reducing taxes, reducing regulation, and rebuilding military strength. Those were simple and well-enunciated goals, and most people could tick off on one hand what President Reagan really wanted to do. That was Ronald Reagan's vision. I think what made him effective is that you knew his core issues and what he hoped to accomplish during the time he was in office. He never lost sight of those goals throughout his presidency. For eight years in office, you can look at almost everything he has done and find one of those key elements that he laid out in the very first days in office.

It is important to a new president and to any president to try to decide the things that you want to do in the first 100 days, set out to accomplish them and show that you are going to grab hold of the controls of government and run it. This is especially true for a Republican president because, with a Congress normally of the other party, there is already an adversarial relationship. Having a Republican Senate when Reagan came in was important in setting out and achieving some of the early goals he wanted to accomplish. The first choice he had to make was whether he should try for economic reform or try to advance the social agenda from the campaign. His advisers, namely, Jim Baker, at this point decided that they were going to use the first 100 days to turn around economic policies in the country and at least subordinate for the time being—not remove, but subordinate—some of the social concerns: school prayer, abortion, things like that. This did not mean that the President would forget about these but that for the first 100 days it was more important to solidify his base for other issues. So in early 1981, President Reagan did go out and cut taxes and tried to get a handle on the spending priorities.

Some of the things that he did in moving those policies are interesting. He used addresses from the Oval Office to speak above the heads of Congress and go directly to the American people in order to build on the mandate that he felt was out there in 1981.

He assumed that the American people were ready for change. To make this change happen he said, "I want the public to rise up and to tell your congressman this is what we want to happen." It also gave him a chance to talk above the press, to talk "unfiltered," as I call it. It was the President not being filtered by a TV camera or by a reporter standing up and saying this is what the President meant to say. Reagan was delivering his whole message to the American people so that they could hear it, understand it, and then decide whether to support what he wanted to do. This was different from having a news reporter in a 30- or 60-second news brief summarize what he said. I think that Oval Office address was important in achieving his early goals and objectives.

It was also useful on the tax cuts. President Reagan constantly referred back to what President Kennedy had done when he was in office, namely that Kennedy had passed the last round of tax cuts in this country. This took away some of the political sting from the Democrats. He was saying, "Wait a minute, if it was OK when President Kennedy did it, it's OK now for this Republican president." It was an interesting use of a previous president and a previous president's objectives to achieve a modern objective. It took away successfully part of the opposition's argument.

There was a second issue, though, that he got into in which he wasn't as successful. This was Social Security, and it still troubles Republicans even today. Last week the Bush campaign was battening down the hatches as Governor Michael Dukakis [D-Mass.] prepared to raise the Social Security issue one more time and claim that the Republicans were going to try to balance the budget on the back of the Social Security recipients in this country. David Stockman had proposed in 1981 that the President should go after the minimum benefit, which was Social Security, for those who never paid into the system. I recall Senator Howard Baker [R-Tenn.] and Congressman Robert Michel [R-Ill.] going into the Oval Office and seeing the President pull out a yellow sheet of paper on which he had written two pages of what he wanted to say on Social Security. The President was going to have a televised address to the American people. Fortunately, he changed his mind because clearly this was not an issue in which he was in control, could drive the agenda, or could win.

I think we learned one thing from Vietnam: If you've got a policy that you care a lot about, go out there and try to convince a majority of the American people to support you. But be careful that you don't lose sight of where the public is and what the public expects. If you have an issue that is so divisive that you will end up losing in the long term, the loss will not be just that issue but other things that you want to accomplish because of the lack of public confidence in your leadership. I think that's what happened to President Johnson. When you look back at the Vietnam War, the objectives laid out were never clearly enunciated, and people could not grab hold of Johnson's agenda and support what he wanted to do. In the case of Social Security, there was no way you could convince the American people at that time, in that heated political environment, that we should go out and do anything negative with Social Security. There has to be an extensive bipartisan education process before you can finally deal with it.

Those are two things in that first year that I think give you an idea of what this President was trying to achieve and the priorities that he set. In doing these, not only did he try to lead the Congress, but he also used the Oval Office address and the direct appeal to the American people to build up support to make these things happen.

Let's look now at the last two years and what we walked into when we got to the White House in February of 1987. To put things in perspective, you have to go back to November 1986. Two events occurred that had a dramatic impact on this presidency during that period in time. Iran-contra is the one everybody refers to, but there is a second one which I think was just as important, and that was the midterm elections in 1986. I ran the Republican Senate Campaign Committee in 1985 and 1986, so I got to sit there and watch as senator after senator on the Republican side went down in defeat. That event changed the perception of who was going to run Washington, who was going to govern, because for the first time since he had been in office, President Reagan was going to have a Congress totally controlled by the other party. I don't think that the President's successes in 1981 would have been as readily achievable if there had not been at least one of the houses of Congress controlled by the Republicans. It gave him time to make the initial offer, have one house carry it, and then come in at the end and put on the final touches. When the elections in 1986 were over, the President not only had to initiate, he also had to carry the battle to the Hill. No longer did he have one of the houses controlled by his party to carry that first line of attack for him. So I believe that was a very significant event.

At that time, the questions in Washington, particularly in the press, were: Is the Congress going to once again control the agenda? Are they going to be deciding the things that are going to happen in Washington, the policies the government is going to follow? Or is the President still going to be a major player? Couple that with the serious political problem the President walked into with the Iran-contra affair, and you can get a good idea of what was going on in the beginning of 1987.

The *Washington Post* wrote several times that the question was whether this President was still going to be able to govern, or whether we were going to basically leave the presidency on hold until the national election in November of 1988.

We came into an administration in which the President's ability to communicate had a strong impact in directing the country, whether it was to achieve budget cuts, tax cuts, or during a major disaster. President Reagan could come out and calm the waters. He could talk about it, bring people together to understand why things happened. The President's voice—and Dick Wirthlin's survey research supports this—added a lot to the public understanding and subsequently the public reaction to what the President wanted to achieve. The decision to remove him from that process, as happened from sometime after mid-November until sometime in March, led to concern and confusion. People wondered if there was more to the Iran-contra problem than on the surface. Why is the President not out there as he had been in the past telling us everything is going to be OK? I think his voice being removed from this public debate really left a void. Any time you have that, there is always enough noise in Washington to fill such a void, and it got filled. In the ensuing days a perception was created that there must be more to this problem then was evident. At the same time the President had undergone surgery, which raised another concern that maybe he was more impaired than the public had been told. Why else would the President, the man who has been there in good times and bad, not be available during this time when we really need him? So that is what we walked into, a White House groping for a mission, for a role, for a president, trying to figure out where it was going to go. The question was: Was this President still going to be able to drive the agenda?

There was one event which occurred within the first day or two after we went to the White House that has stayed in my mind over these past months. I was sitting in the Roosevelt Room on that Saturday, which was 28 February 1987, at a table almost the size of this one, full of White House aides who were preparing the President for his first national address in four months to talk about the Iran-contra affair. I was at the far end with Jim Cannon, who was also part of the transition team, and we listened as the White House staff talked about the President's address to come the following Wednesday. They knew what time it was going to be, but nobody had any idea what it was he was going to say.

And if you are talking about the great communicator, one of this President's strengths as a communicator was that he knew before he ever spoke what it was he wanted to say. Only then would the time and the date be set. This occasion was exactly opposite. It was backwards. That told me more than anything else about the internal problems at the White House, and that it was time for a change in the staff arrangement. The President often went out, ran this country through problem after problem, laid out objectives and goals, and achieved them. The staff was prepared to toss him out there and worry later about what happened. Fortunately, we were able within a few days to pull this together so when the President did make the speech, he talked about mistakes that were made. But this experience told a lot. If you've got a good communicator, as this President was, you don't misuse him. You keep in mind that his strength to communicate is based on knowing when to go out and say something, to provide the leadership for the country, and how to move them to his point of view. However, you don't overuse or misuse this. You don't say, "The only thing we've got is the President; let's just throw him out there and see what happens." I think that was part of what the attitude was in the White House, not because they were trying to hurt him, but because they didn't know what else to do at that point in time.

So we faced not only getting the President through Iran-contra, but also reestablishing his position to deal at least on an even basis with the Congress. We laid out a three-part plan for the remainder of 1987. The first was to recognize during those early spring months that we had to organize how to present the Iran-contra story and how to handle the pending investigations on the Hill.

The second phase took place in the summer. We knew that the Congress would start dealing with the budget and appropriating dollars and things like that. How could the President go back to some of the basics of 1981 to set the agenda? We wanted the message to be, "I've got priorities for spending; here is what we are going to do, and I intend to be part of it." Out of that came the idea of the Economic Bill of Rights.

The third part was the fall agenda which we felt would include a summit of some type with the Soviet Union. For this President it would show that he was in control and in charge if a major adversary of this country was willing to sit down with him and negotiate the first arms control agreement that actually reduced weapons. That's how we approached 1987. There was one overriding theme: For the first two-term president since Eisenhower it was important to make sure that he was part of the agenda in 1988; that George Bush—who most people expected to be the nominee—was not trying to run away from Ronald Reagan but was trying to build on Ronald Reagan; that President Reagan was going to be a factor in 1988; and that his policies, his goals, and his reshaping of the things that government should do, were going to be a very critical part of the 1988 national agenda and would be discussed among the Republican and Democratic candidates for president. The sign to me that we had achieved that goal was the debate held in Washington, D.C., in December 1987, when Senator Paul Simon [D-Ill.] made a proposal for a new program and Senator Albert Gore [D-Tenn.] questioned him, "How are you going to pay for it?" That is not normally the way the Congress deals with problems. They don't ever ask, "How are you going to pay for it?" They spend it and then worry about how they are going to pay for it later. I found it very interesting that the Democratic candidates were talking and quizzing themselves. They said, "If you want to propose, then you've got to figure out how you are going to pay for it." That is something Ronald Reagan has left. His legacy is making us face the problem on the front end. We've still got a long way to go, but at least it changes the debate just a little bit.

That told me more than anything else that this President was going to be a factor in 1988, and I think he is. The goals that he set out in 1981 about the role of government, the role of this country in the world, and the things that we should try to achieve clearly are part of the debate that we are looking at now. This is because the question in 1988 is change. Is it change in which one party advocates going in a different direction, or is it the change that George Bush talks about, which is, "We are the change"? If President Reagan had not been able to bounce back, then I know the change people would support.

Let's look at the summits for a moment because they may be the highlights for this President in the second part of his term. He has had the ability to take the message that he had campaigned on since the mid-1960s, put it on an international stage, and let people look at what he wanted to say and the imprint he wanted to leave. I also think he was able to capture not only the minds of people in this country, but also the minds of people around the world by choosing the images that he wanted to convey in his message, by focusing on individual freedoms, which are the foundation of our country, and by going into audiences that were a little foreign to him. I know the Soviets were curious about why President Reagan wanted to appear at Moscow State University and talk about America, about values, and about changes. But his presentation gave them a view of what freedom and democracy are all about. Our media, a number of whom had never been to the Soviet Union, carefully watched this President as he communicated to those Soviet students and understood that his message was getting through. That is also part of what this President has left: an image of this country in a much broader international scale, so that any candidate who comes after him will have a building point. This President was able, because of things he wanted to do, to communicate that this is a different time and that we've got to figure out how the United States and the Soviet Union can work together to try to lessen the concerns of a nuclear war, and that we are co-trustees of the survival of this world.

I can't tell you how often the press would inquire, "But this is the same man who talked about the evil empire." And I can still see the President sitting next to General Secretary Gorbachev in their first meeting in the Kremlin with Andrea Mitchell of NBC yelling out, "Mr. President, is he still the leader of the evil empire?" The President politely tried to figure out how to respond, and said finally, "Well, things change." The press knew the President's early messages were used to try to get America's military rebuilt back to the point where he thought that we needed to be and then to sit down with the Soviets and deal with them. They lost sight of the fact that President Reagan got criticized quite often in 1981 and 1982 for going forward with INF, and that the Soviets walked away from the negotiating table. There were questions raised over whether it was time for the United States maybe to step back and reassess its position. But he stayed the course, sure of where he wanted to go, so that when he got to that point he could respond, "I'm not saying everything is right in the Soviet Union, but I am saying that there is a difference here and that it is time to figure out what we can do to work with them." With this President, delivering that message is almost as significant as when President Nixon went to China and was able to reestablish U.S.-China relations.

Reagan was the right president to open up a new dialogue with the Soviets. He set the stage early by showing a determination to be strong enough that we could sit down and deal with the Soviets on an equal basis and convince a majority of people in this country that we were not giving away more than we were getting in return. That's communication, but it is also leadership, and that's what this President has been able to do: to take words, policies, and direction and transfer them into goals and leadership for this country. Part of what he will leave behind is this new relationship with the Soviets and the different concept of the role of government. But also what he will leave behind for his successor is proven communication skills as tools of leadership. How do you work with a media that is always searching and probing to figure out why you made a certain decision or why certain things happen? What is the presidential role in "orchestrating a message"?

I don't think there is anything wrong with a president having the opportunity to at least let the people know what he is trying to do; the media is going to tell people what they think he is trying to do. Part of his job is trying to get out some flavor for and some sense of his overall goals. But in trying to get your message out, you must also recognize the right of the people to know so that they can be informed about decisions that are being made. This means that there has to be a relationship between a president of the United States and the media that cover him daily at the White House. The next president needs to really look long and hard at how to work with the media, how to take some of the tension out of the relationship. He will also have to determine how to impress on the White House press corps that with the right they have to cover a president also comes responsibility, that the words shown on the air or written in the newspaper, many times, are all that most people are going to know about the public policy decisions.

Hopefully, one of the first acts of any new administration will be to figure out how best to communicate their goals, hopes, and desires through the press as the available outlet to tell all of us what the administration wants to do. If the press decides not to cooperate, then the president has to find other communication outlets. However, a president cannot stay above the press for very long, because the press is the way the majority of people in this country receive information used to shape public attitudes.

Let me conclude with just a couple of points. I think it is important for a president, when he goes in, to know what he wants to do and to set out to try to accomplish it, to have a clear set of goals, to be concise in laying them out, and to try to build toward accomplishing those things he wants to see happen. A president needs a vision and really needs to understand how he best conveys the direction he wants to offer the people of America. He also needs to recognize that people look at a president in a different light. A president is more than just someone who is elected to office: he is the figurehead who represents the hopes, dreams, and future of this country.

However, part of his responsibility is to recognize that he must work with the institutions that exist. He also must ensure that people understand and appreciate what he wants to do, and that he is available to them not only when things are good, but also when things are bad. The president must provide leadership by being a president of all the people all the time. The president must also communicate his goals to a public waiting to know, and he must do it within the framework that we provide in this country—the news media.

NARRATOR: When Tom Griscom was Senator Howard Baker's press secretary, he had a double recognition. One, he was considered the best press secretary on Capitol Hill by many people. Two, Senator Baker used to say that more people came to hear Tom Griscom's press conferences than they did Senator Baker's. We now have an opportunity to test whether or not Senator Baker is correct.

QUESTION: You talk about the president's need to use the press to get his message across to the people, and yet this President has probably had fewer press conferences than any president in recent history. I mention this because this Center eight years ago came out with a report on presidential press conferences which advocated having at least one a month. I don't know when President Reagan last had a press conference, but I would guess it was probably some time last spring.

TOM GRISCOM: I will see if I can remember when it was because we did it. You can tell that there is a presidential campaign going on because we have lost the constant badgering about having a press conference, once the focus turned outside of the White House. I think that this administration made a mistake early on in trying to turn the press conference into a prime-time event, an entertainment event, if I may be so bold as to call it that.

One of the things we talked about when we came to the White House was going back to the notion of doing press conferences at 2 or 3 o'clock in the afternoon. Why do they all have to be 8 o'clock at night? The argument that came back was: "Well, we want to make sure that the maximum number of people see the President. But we also want to do it so that we can say what we want to unfiltered rather than saying it in the afternoon, letting the networks decide whether to show this piece or that and watching them analyze his comments from the afternoon."

To tell you the truth, I really got tired of those people saying that a president should be infallible. I think one of the things about this President that has been very beneficial to the country and to him is the recognition that he does make mistakes. He misstates himself and will make an error here or there, but that's what humans do. We make mistakes all the time; we learn from our mistakes. So why are we trying to create an image of a president who never makes a mistake? I think that's what some of them were trying to do. They said, "We are going to save him from himself." Well, I found this President was a lot brighter, a lot sharper than many half of his age.

But, to go back to your point, I agree with you. I think a press conference is an integral part of the presidency. I don't think it is the only way, though, for a president to communicate. What I would hope that we see when this presidency is over and the next one comes in is a revision of the press conference in light of a couple of thoughts. First, when we were in the Senate, the two leaders of the Senate each morning started off their day by bringing the press onto the floor of the Senate and talking to them for about five or ten minutes about what the agenda was for that day, or whatever might be on their mind. I'd like to see the president start his day that way. He could bring in 10 or 15 reporters each morning and talk about what's going on that particular day. Is there going to be a specific meeting that he is going to attend? Is there something he wants to lay out to set the tone? However, these should not be set in an environment where the president is sitting there and everybody is trying to test him and see if they can get him to make a mistake.

Second, get out of this idea that press conferences have to be at 8 o'clock at night. Go back to afternoon press conferences, or at least alternate them half and half. You are making it a major event by doing it at 8 o'clock in the evening. You are allowing the Dan Rathers to say that whether a president can get through a press conference determines whether he can still govern or not. That, to me, is nothing short of incredible, that anyone would even think that a press conference takes on that magnitude. Switching the time also does one other thing: it might help us get away from the idea that the reporters, particularly TV correspondents, have to become stars in their own right. To them it is very important to be able to stand up and have their name shown on the screen—that this is so-and-so with ABC News—and to throw the question that might stump the President that night. With a different time we would get out of this thing where the people who are covering the news actually become the news themselves.

I noticed when we would travel around various places in this country that one TV correspondent worked the crowd before the President made his speech. That's what we created. The prime time news conference created that, and I think that's wrong.

One last point: The President would probably get better questions if we alternated press conferences in Washington with press conferences in other places in the country. At a press conference in Chicago or Los Angeles or Boston or wherever, you get different types of questions than those asked by persons who are so trapped inside of Washington that all they think about is what is driving that city. It is refreshing to go to another place and find out what it is that worries America, because quite often it's not what worries Washington. It would be very refreshing to start this and at least be able to take press conferences outside the White House and the White House press corps.

Now if we did all this, the White House press corps would come up and say, "No, you can't do that. We are charged by our news organizations to cover the president." Fine, they can be there, but I don't think anybody says they have the exclusive right to ask the only questions of the President of the United States. We get the argument that "If we can't have our cameras there all the time, then we are just not going to cover him." I say, "That's fine, because I don't think a network correspondent would last very long if he can't get on TV." In a word, the president should be willing to come back and play hardball the other way. Too often there is the tendency to criticize and ridicule the press for what they do, but then nobody wants to risk their wrath by deciding to do things a little bit differently. It's much easier to criticize than to try to offer a solution to the problem.

As I said, I hope that whoever is in the White House next would spend some time on reestablishing contact with the media, recognizing fully that there are times when he cannot sit down and answer specific questions on the record. We did make a conscious decision in May of last year [1987] not to do a press conference, and we were under pressure from the media because they wanted to ask the President questions about the Iran-contra affair. However, he decided a part of our job was to keep the inquiry on the Hill in the hearing room and not bring it inside the White House. We also decided not to put a president in front of the press only to have his White House legal counsel instruct him, "Mr. President, you can't answer that. You've got to say 'I cannot comment.'" I think a previous president made the line "I cannot comment" an unacceptable line in this country for it sounds like you are hiding something. We chose not to have a press conference last May, but in making that choice, did that mean that we could not do other things? The answer was no. You have to be flexible enough to recognize that there is a role for the press, a responsibility to let the American people know and get a sense of what is going on. I hope the next president and the press sit down and learn from what I think were some of the mistakes that were made.

QUESTION: Mr. Griscom, I'd like to ask you a question having basically two parts. One concerns the word "interface," and the other concerns the word "charismatic." Would you comment on your relationship as a speech writer with the President in formulating ideas? What freedom do you feel when the President makes a suggestion to his advisers that runs contrary to your feelings, or which you disagree with? And on the other hand, what freedom do you have to make suggestions in selling the idea to the President? Also, you have been so effective at this that you've made the President of the United States achieve such great skill in the use of charisma that it is going to be exceedingly difficult for his successors to measure up to the standards that you have been so helpful in setting. Would you comment on that?

TOM GRISCOM: Let me answer the last part first. I hope that people measure George Bush and Mike Dukakis by their standard. I understand that they are measured up against this President. But if we get to a situation where the person has to meet the job rather than the job meeting the person, then I think we need to reassess how we make decisions in this country. Each president ought to be different; each president ought to draw on his strengths for the office. For this President it was important for him to be able as a public figure to set the agenda, and he did it as a communicator. That was his leadership tool, being able to go out and rally the people for a particular point of view. Each president is not going to have that same ability. Another president might be much more capable of sitting down with Congress and putting together a coalition that leads the country. So I hope that we don't get so caught up that the measuring stick becomes this President.

I mentioned to Senator Baker when he was still thinking about running for president, that I thought whoever the next president is, he needs to define the office post-Reagan. And I don't think either Bush or Dukakis has defined the office yet for what it is that they want to do post-Reagan. I hope that they do that over the next five weeks, because they have got to give people an idea of what they want to achieve. They have to build on their predecessor and tell us what the things are that they want to do. If they don't, then I think what you say is exactly right. There will be a tendency to use this President as a measuring stick, and when the future president gets up and can't make a good public speech, people are going to say, "Boy, he must be a failure." So I think it is important for the candidates to sketch out what they would do and how they want to put the office together.

Now let me go to the first part of your question. A lot of people don't realize that this President is a very good editor and writer in his own right. When he was on the mashed potato circuit when he did the radio program after his unsuccessful bid for president in 1976, and before he ran in 1980, he wrote his own speeches. He wrote those radio addresses. If I had a problem with a speech where I couldn't get it sweated out, I'd send it to the President, and he would sit down and edit it. He was one of the best editors. But I did not do that too often because there just was not enough time for him to spend on that.

I think part of what we brought to the White House in the final two years of the second term that maybe was missing with some of the previous occupants who were there before us was a good staff. I think any president needs a good staff; it is a question of how much staff is needed and what the role of that staff is. President Reagan had a clear set of goals he wanted to accomplish. However, he would delegate a lot of the authority and a lot of the implementation of those goals and objectives. To do this successfully requires that he have people who are serving him, who understand him and his way of governing. It is what I call the Howard Baker rule of "no surprises," which means that if I am going to go out and perform my responsibilities, I need to make sure that the President never gets blindsided. I need at least to have given him an idea of where I am heading with something so that he is not surprised at some point and says, "I wish they had told me about this."

As for putting together speeches, let me use the summit, if I may; it is probably the best example. We went in to talk to the President for the first time about the Moscow summit speeches back in February of this year. Remember, the summit was at the end of May. We started planning for the Moscow summit or the possibility that there would be a summit within a week after the Washington summit ended. What we did was to look at what we had done in Washington and at what this President had done over the years in formulating his relationship with the Soviet Union. We went out and put some concepts together and did some survey research work. We also used some focus groups to basically test the notions that we thought might work. We did this before we talked to the President—I'll be honest with you. But then before we went any further, we took these ideas in and sat down with him and said, "In planning for a possible trip to the Soviet Union, we would like you to consider these themes." He spent two or three days, sent them back to us, and said, "These are OK; go ahead."

The President was accessible all the way through this process. The speech writers came in and sat down with him for a couple of sessions, because this President can come up with one or two phrases that become very integral to a speech and that make the speech. But you don't get that unless you sit down and walk through it with him. The best speech writer in the world can craft the words, but you lose that personal touch unless you talk to the principal. So we talked with him on several occasions. We also made sure that the Moscow speeches went to President Reagan about three and a half weeks before the event, so that he had a chance to read them, to revise them, and to make sure we hadn't missed the mark. Going over the speeches once more, he made sure that we studied the overview that we had used when we first sat down and talked to him about what we all wanted to achieve—the broad message of individual freedom and the idea that we are building on a relationship for the future. So President Reagan had in front of him all the concepts that we had talked about in building these speeches.

He also had a list of all the events that we were planning and the various meeting groups. For example, when we decided to meet writers and filmmakers, the goal was to carry the theme of individual freedom. We told the President that what he should relate was his own experience as an actor in Hollywood, because the Soviets had a tough time figuring out how an actor ever got to be President of the United States. In their country an actor could never be anything but an actor. One of the things for him to personalize for them was how somebody in his profession could also get into public service, and how this country allows that kind of freedom. We tried to bridge all these images and things into that overall message of individual freedom. That is how we put those speeches together. We captured the essence of the things that he wanted; we looked at the event for which we had to put the speech together; and we gave him enough time to go through the speeches and make sure they made the points that he wanted. That is the process we went through, whether it was the Moscow summit or the State of the Union Address.

Let me give you one other example. I don't know how many of you recall when the President dropped the prop, the big appropriation bill, in the State of the Union Address. I will put my modesty aside for a minute; that was my idea, so I'm going to take full credit for it because I thought it worked pretty well. We knew with this President that he had the ability to take a visual like that and make an impact on the spoken word, that he could make it happen. In working on that speech we sat down with him about ten days before it was to be given. We already had the speech basically closed. However, we wanted to drive home the point that the budget process was out of control and had to be fixed; that we could no longer sit back on Christmas Eve and be signing a $600 billion spending bill, that this had to change. That is when we came up with a visual to make this point. We went in there and rehearsed this visual aid with President Reagan twice, and he didn't drop it on his finger when he rehearsed it. That is what we went through with this President so that he was comfortable with it, but also so that he didn't feel like that it was demeaning or took away from what he wanted to say. I use that as a second example.

We made a point of trying to work with him so that anything we did, did not lose what I call the Reagan touch, because he had such an ability to take that written word and bring it off the paper. We never wanted to lose sight of building on that strength that he had.

NARRATOR: Could you say anything about how you interface—to use Mr. Newman's words—with the diplomatic and security people? Did you talk with George Shultz or with anyone else as you went along?

TOM GRISCOM: I've got all the scars and bruises. I used to be six feet tall. This is how I ended up five feet, six inches. I got chopped down a little bit at a time. What the White House requires is that a chief of staff really ought to be a chief of staff, which means he ought to have the ability to control and direct people who work for the president. Right now it is not necessarily an all-encompassing position.

If there is a presidential summit, then the White House has to be in the position to direct the summit and to make the decisions, because somebody has to coordinate the Defense Department, the NSC, the State Department, the CIA, and all the other people who get involved at a summit. You have got to have one person in charge. This is what I think went wrong with Iran-contra. There was not one person who remained in charge throughout that process, and people started filling the void. Part of what I had to do, along with General Colin Powell, was to be the White House summit team. Our responsibility was to coordinate. If we had a speech problem, which we had a couple of times, particularly for the speech in Finlandia Hall, it had to be resolved. The speech writer and the State Department human rights person often got going in circles, so I brought them in on a Saturday, sat down with them, and we worked it out. We were able to do that because they understood that my position gave me the final word on presidential speech text. I gave everybody a chance to air their points and concerns, but they finally had to come to closure.

Whether it's that case or something else, there always has to be somebody in charge, somebody who is going to take the responsibility. If the summit in Moscow had failed, I recognized that I was going to be the person who was going to take the hits. That is part of the responsibility that you assume, I think, no matter whether it is government service or if you work for a business. If you are going to be responsible, take it and be willing to take the good with the bad, but also realize when the time comes for closure on something, do it and get it moving down the road.

QUESTION: Let's go back to 1981. No one doubts that President Reagan had a mission and a message that he wanted to translate into legislation, and he accomplished that. But there is some question in political science of whether he had a mandate. Some people say that he went to Capitol Hill and the press in 1981 and was able to convince them, partially on the strength that the American people were behind him. Other people say that actually he convinced Congress and the press first and that the American people were the last to be convinced. It was the press, after all, that came up with the term "the great communicator," not the Reagan White House. This view argues that Ronald Reagan impressed people inside the Beltway first. He was not Jimmy Carter: he could work with people, was a decent fellow, and had an idea of what he wanted to do. The American people came along only after Washington did. What do you think of that controversy?

TOM GRISCOM: I would take the other side of it because I think what you remember is that when he was struggling to get some of the tax cuts through, he went out to the public and then they brought the pressure back to the Hill by saying, "Call your congressman." However, several other times when Reagan said, "Call your congressman," it didn't happen. Then Jim Wright or somebody would say, "Well, the President made an appeal and nobody called us this time." The term "the great communicator," I agree with you, wasn't a White House term; it was a press term, just like "Reaganomics" was a press term. But I think he got the name "the great communicator" because he was able to communicate a message to the majority of the people in this country and get the "silent majority" to do something, to get them up to the point where they felt enough concern to support what he was trying to do and to actually make a phone call. This has not happened very often. You find the majority of people in this country do not like to get involved.

Yes, I think he was able to work within the Beltway, but I think he was also able to use the public to let the Beltway understand that there were people out there who were behind what he was trying to do. Having spent ten years in Washington and having been involved on the Hill, I have noticed that Congress reacts to the moment quite often. If something is happening today they want to deal with it, but if all of a sudden it shifts some place else they are going to shift along with it. The fact that you could use the public to help keep Congress focused was an ability that Reagan was able to draw on. It didn't last forever. Once things moved and once the recession ended and things started going ahead, then when he made the calls to do this or that, you didn't find the same level of support. Does that mean the mandate was gone? No, I think the mandate was still there because Congress did not come behind it and undo everything he tried to do. But I do think he was able to capture in those first 100 days the momentum that he had coming out of the election and going into office, and he used it to complement the things he wanted to accomplish. So I do think there was public input, because Congress will respond if they get enough phone calls and enough letters. Remember when the President put the coalition together in the House with the boll weevils and the gypsy moths. At that time you had Speaker O'Neill, who was out there trying to win because Tip O'Neill did not like to lose. President Reagan was able to succeed because he could show that there was public support for what he was trying to accomplish, and therefore Congress went along with it as long as that public support was there. When the election in 1982 went the other way, that's when you found the boll weevils and gypsy moths coming back home, because they felt the public had basically said in 1982, "This President has done all he really needs to do in changing the economic factors in this country; let's ease off a little bit." Then it became much more of a maintenance process than trying to make fundamental changes any more.

QUESTION: Mr. Griscom, you said that one of Ronald Reagan's legacies was "pay as you go." You also indicated that he doesn't like to back losing issues. As Mr. Mondale found out, "pay as you go" is a losing issue. Is the President's legacy what he says or what he does?

TOM GRISCOM: I think it is a little bit of each. I knew when I said "pay as you go" I was in trouble because I should have clarified the point I was trying to make. I was not trying to dismiss the deficit, which requires our attention. The next president has some very tough choices to make. He is going to have to be able to portray himself to this country as one who can be trusted and can figure out how to generate bipartisan support in Congress to achieve the things that are going to be necessary to get a handle on the deficit.

By "pay as you go," the point I was trying to make was this: You can no longer just say, "Well, let's do this and not worry about either where the money is going to come from or whether we are going to have to take away from another program or shift priorities." If we suddenly decide that we are going to have a larger defense program, we are going to have to figure out now how we are going to pay for it. Are we going to take it out of social programs? Or are we going to have to make some reductions in the military programs in this country to be able to provide the services and other things that people want? Or are we going to be able to go out and convince the people that there ought to be a new tax to pay for what it is that they want done? I think all of those questions are out there. I think that the tax question is very much going to be part of what the next president has to deal with.

I think the dreaded "T" word is going to raise its head several times because that is also part of "pay as you go," from my way of thinking. I think if you convince people that there is a reason for a particular program or budget decision, you must show them why new revenues may be necessary to make it happen. That is part of the responsibility that the next president is going to have. But that is also part of "pay as you go." The next president needs to tell people up front what they are getting and why they are getting it. He should try to see if he can rally the country to support what it is that he wants to do. They may say they don't want that, and that's part of the public debate. I think that just going out and saying, "We're going to create a massive new program," while not worrying about the impact that it will have or whether it takes away from this or that part of the budget, is an option that no longer exists. Now you must at least look at how it balances off against other spending priorities in the budget. That's my point.

I did not mean to deflect the deficit question, which is a major problem facing the next president. It will require the executive and legislative branches to declare a truce with each other, sit down together, stop finger pointing, and figure out what they can do to get our accounts back towards some type of balance.

QUESTION: I might just observe that at the start this President did raise taxes rather substantially, particularly in Social Security, and that, to some extent, camouflages the depth of the crisis on the budget. What happened to the President's ability to communicate his ideas effectively when he campaigned for several senators who did not win in 1986?

TOM GRISCOM: Let me tell you what happened. I appreciate your raising that. There was a real effort to try to figure out what the message to the country in 1986 should be. I always worried, when this President got reelected in 1984, that he got reelected on the fact that Walter Mondale was talking about raising taxes and things like that. The President never really clearly laid out what it was that he wanted to do in the second four years. Getting an arms control agreement was part of it, but when you are dealing with a foreign policy issue it is much harder to focus the agenda than it is when you are dealing with the domestic issue. After the election was over in 1984, there were a lot of questions. What is the administration going to do? Getting an arms control agreement is important, but what else are you going to do for four years? There was a void, and suddenly tax reform emerged. Then the competitiveness idea was developed. Clearly the last four years were designed for foreign policy achievements and for an arms control agreement. The domestic agenda did not produce the same punch.

What happened in 1986? Knowing that there was no clearly defined message, the Republican party said, "OK, we need to go back and remind the American people how things were." Well, Americans, I found, do not like to be reminded of things that weren't good. I think that's also what Republicans have faced in 1988. How do they repackage without looking like they are bashing Jimmy Carter? Inflation was here, interest rates were here, and unemployment was here. How do they throw the misery index back out there and make people try to remember that things weren't so good? That's when you get the Bush idea that "we are a party of change." They have been trying for two years to figure out how to remind people of what they were like eight years ago, because that is a long time for Americans to remember things. You don't want to have to think back when things weren't necessarily good.

So part of the problem in 1986 was figuring out what the message should be. There was an internal struggle going on with the conservatives who were saying, "This ought to be a time to throw the gauntlet down and to say that we are going to lay out these points, we are going to campaign on this agenda," whether it was abortion, support for the contras, or whatever. If you notice, though, those issues are not where the majority of the people are. They do not want to be pulled apart by those kind of divisive issues in an off-year election.

The second problem was the way the message was finally positioned. The President's message ended up saying, "You support me and Senator X, and that is a sign that you support the contras." Clearly at that point, at best, the contras were a 50-50 issue. It is not that now, but then, at best, it was 50-50. Reagan's message was: Vote for Senator—let's say Mattingly—because it's a vote for me.

That is the wrong way to package that kind of a message. It should have been "Vote for Mack Mattingly because he has been important for this, this, and this to happen, and that has produced these results," rather than, "Vote for Mattingly because I need him back." People did not respond well to that message at all. They said, "That's fine, Mr. President, but what has he done for us?" The message did not say what these individual senators in a six-year period have really done for their constituents back home. It was not packaged right. I will tell you I do not know how I would have been able to go back and change it, because there were many factions that were fighting against each other trying to capture the message. The White House clearly wanted to turn it into a referendum on the President. That was a mistake, because then they were running on national issues which, as I said, were clearly not 70 or 80 percent approval issues. If you had 70 or 80 percent approval, that would have been different, but when you are running on issues that, at best, are 50-50 then you are forcing people to struggle with their decision. They say, "Well, do I really want this? I'm not sure I want to support the freedom fighters in Nicaragua."

There is one image that has stayed in my mind from the 1986 election, and that was Senator Jim Abdnor, who was in a debate in South Dakota. A question came up: "Senator, can you explain to me why you sent $100 million to Nicaragua, and we've got farmers who are just in ruin in our country?" He didn't have an answer. Finally, what he came up with was, "Well, the President asked me to do it," and that just didn't sell back home. It just didn't make it. What happened is that it turned into a national referendum on the President's policies. In doing that it gave the Democrats the ability to bring out voters who might not have come out otherwise, because clearly the issues that were being constructed as part of that national agenda were not 70 or 80 percent approval issues. They were very cutting issues, and it got into a litmus test. That was not the way to run it.

QUESTION: I think I heard you early in your talk agreeing with the conventional wisdom that LBJ did not successfully enunciate our aims in Vietnam. My question is whether you think Reagan has better enunciated our aims in Nicaragua than Johnson did in Vietnam.

TOM GRISCOM: No, I do not, and let me tell you why. I go back to my days in the Senate with Senator Baker. I think there were two or three different messages they were trying to put out there. I think the President knew what he wanted to do, but I don't think it ever filtered down to the staff that had to implement it. I think there were some within the State Department who wanted to overthrow that government, and some, including the secretary of state, who wanted to figure out how to at least deal with the region and put something together that would bring some democratic reform into Central America. There were others who just said, "Let's just leave it alone. We haven't been able to do anything with these people for years, so why do we want to get in the middle of it now?"

You had three different things going on. I think those three things ended up making an Iran-contra happen, because one of the people involved in one of those three elements came to the top. He decided, "If nobody else is going to lead, I'll lead it," and he did. He grabbed hold of it and tried to move forward. I think that clearly was part of the situation that was there.

The President never fully enunciated what the goals and aspirations were that he wanted to achieve in Central America. Look at the message. When you talked about a Soviet beachhead, the approval rating was 80 percent: No, we don't want the Soviets to have a beachhead in Central America. But then when you talked about wanting the contras to overthrow the Sandinista government, the polls were 30-60 against. It depended on how you positioned it. There were those who always said, "Well, let's go and put the President out one more time, and we are going to use the line 'Soviet beachhead'." Well, that's fine until people start looking behind it and saying, "Wait a minute, that's not what we are talking about. Let's talk about what's a contra and what's a Sandinista." If you recall, they finally started referring to contras as freedom fighters, because otherwise you didn't know whether a contra was a good guy or a bad guy. So you started trying to call them freedom fighters, and you started mixing up whether a freedom fighter was a contra or whatever. It brought a sense of confusion. I agree with you. It is on a different scale from Vietnam, because we have not committed American troops into Central America as we had in Vietnam. The public was not clearly in a place to understand what the objectives were, what we were trying to achieve down there, and how we were going to set about doing it. We did not have the ability when we came into the White House to undo the previous five years because it was very confused, and people just could not really sort out why this mattered and why it was important.

No, I don't argue that point at all. I think it was not handled well. If the goal was to overthrow the Sandinistas, then we should have flat said that. I don't think that was the President's goal, but if that is what he really wanted to do, he should have said, "Here's what we are going to do," and then drive toward that goal. Or if the goal was to try to make the Sandinistas more willing to work with the other countries in Central America, then lay that out and drive toward that goal. But I think it was a very confused message that was not well enunciated. People really were trying to figure out why we were down there. When only 30 percent of the people in this country even knew where Nicaragua is, they should have realized that the administration hadn't done something right. I think that is still the right number: Only 30 percent of the people know where it is, and some people even thought it was a part of the United States. That tells you that the administration did not achieve its goal of driving public opinion to support the policy in Central America.

NARRATOR: According to my figures, at 38 years of age, Tom Griscom has at least 32 years left to return to the University of Virginia periodically. Those of you who have heard him will be as anxious as I in the years ahead to hear what he has to say. It is a great pleasure to have you with us.

CHAPTER 3

THE REAGAN PRESIDENCY: ATOP THE SECOND TIER

DONALD THOMAS REGAN

NARRATOR: From 1981 to 1985 Donald Regan was secretary of the treasury and thereafter chief of staff to President Reagan. Donald Regan is the author of *A View from the Street*; he was a trustee of the Charles Merrill Trust; he rose in the ranks as secretary and director of the administrative division, then executive vice president, president, and finally chairman and chief executive officer of Merrill Lynch, Pierce, Fenner & Smith and its predecessors. He has been chairman of the board and life trustee of the University of Pennsylvania, a member of the policy committee of the Business Roundtable, and a trustee of the Committee for Economic Development. He fought in at least five major campaigns in the Pacific and rose to the rank of lieutenant colonel in the U. S. Marine Corps. It is a great privilege to have him in the Miller Center oral history on the Reagan presidency.

MR. REGAN: Thank you for that nice introduction. I am fascinated by this project that you are embarking on—the study of the Reagan presidency—because it has baffled so many people. It has confounded his opponents, and it is unexplainable to many intellectuals how this Hollywood actor could have done what he has done and gotten away with it. They simply cannot understand it. Let me try to explain a little bit about it from my particular vantage point as a financier with no political background joining an administration of very skilled politicians and witnessing what happened during that time.

Ronald Reagan, in my judgment, will go down in history, if not in the top tier, then certainly at the top of the second tier among presidents of the United States since World War I. With the exceptions of Roosevelt and Truman, and possibly one or two others, few will have accomplished as much as this man in his eight-year term. Of course, we are still living during that time, and for that reason, to many it is hard to see Reagan in this light. We do not have the luxury of 20-20 hindsight and being able to look back on today to say they did this right or they didn't do that right.

But, from the point of view of Ronald Reagan, all you have to do is to start ticking off some of his accomplishments to get the scope of what I think his legacy will be. First, let's take the domestic side. Now I know there are many who will agree and many who will disagree with my next statements. But for the moment consider them as the truth. I will debate the points later. First, Ronald Reagan did inherit a domestic economic mess. I was on Wall Street at the time and I can assure you that in 1979 and 1980 the stock market and the bond market were close to panic. We had a prime lending rate of up to 21 percent at its peak. Why? Because inflation was rising so much and bankers—as all good bankers do—were demanding a better price for their money at a time of spiraling inflation. Inflation was running 11, 12, 13 percent. It hit an almost 17 percent annual rate at one point.

Paul Volcker had panicked in 1979 at an international banker's conference, raced back to the United States, and put on the brakes; so much so that we all went over the rail, hit the bottom, and we had a recession in 1980. True, it was short-lived, but nevertheless it caused great consternation: a recession in the middle of a presidential campaign. From the point of view of the Carter people it was, "Thanks a lot, Paul," for the great present that you gave the President.

The reversal of the recession, again, was short-lived. The Fed pumped in money, the economy took off for a while, but by putting the monetary brakes on again so tightly Volcker created the recession of 1981 and 1982. That recession ended in November of 1982, and we've had an expansion ever since. This is the longest up leg on a business cycle in peacetime since the 1920s. We've had prosperity for six years with a promise—at least according to all the pundits at this point—that it's going to continue for some months to come.

By the way, a caution here for those of you who are worried about your investments; things always come to a conclusion. Trees don't grow to the sky, and this economic cycle will end. One of the first jobs of the next president, regardless of who he may be, is to figure out how to stave off the oncoming recession. At the current moment it looks like the recession should be a minor one rather than a major one, but nevertheless it has to come in the next presidency.

How did the Reagan era expansion happen and why, in view of the huge deficits in the budget and trade account? In spite of those deficits, we managed to have the lowest unemployment rate in 15 years, to have more people at work than any time in our history, and to have people generally—not all, but *generally*—better off than they have been in many years. That's one of Reagan's major economic accomplishments.

The second item on the domestic front is that he certainly has changed the tax code (for better, or worse, depending upon whether you enjoy tax shelters), in my judgment at least, to be fairer. Many people have been taken off the tax rolls at the lower end of the scale. I think from that point of view it is a better tax code today, if a tax code can ever be considered a good tax code, than it has been for decades. In spite of a lot of charges about what Reagan has done or not done on the domestic scene, whether he has spent enough money on education, or social welfare, or medicine, or what have you, I believe that we are doing well in most of those areas. Maybe we are not as well off as many people would like, but nevertheless a lot of money has been spent on those projects.

On the international scene, his accomplishments are truly of historical note. The fact that this movie idol could meet with the dashing, brilliant, dynamic leader of communism and accomplish so much, again has confounded people. But look what has happened. We all know about the INF Treaty; we know that we are further down the road on the START talks; and we know that relationships with the Soviets are much better today than they have been in the past 30 or 40 years. Not to say that they are perfect—they aren't. I doubt if they ever will be as long as the Soviets are devoted, as they are, to their brand of government. But from the point of view of the world itself, look at what has happened in the regional areas. This is an accomplishment for which Reagan so far has been given very little credit, if any, by the pundits, both in the media and in academia.

One of the first things we did when we were thinking about what our agenda would be for Geneva was to put regional problems very high on the list. Take a look at what has happened in the three years since 1985. The Soviets are just about out of Afghanistan and are committed to getting out. So that bloody war has an ending that has surprised everybody—a Soviet pullout. Secondly, we are engaged in talks concerning Angola. Whether or not these will lead to a conclusion, I don't know, but certainly the impetus is there for a Cuban pullout because the Soviets are no longer backing them and do not want to back them to the extent they had been during the 1960s, 1970s, and the early 1980s. In Nicaragua tensions have lessened. I don't like the way it is entering its current stage—with a whimper rather than a bang—but nevertheless, be that as it may, the tensions have been lowered there. In Vietnam, certainly tensions have been lowered. And in the Middle East, tensions have also been reduced. You may not think so looking at Israel, the West Bank, and Gaza, but certainly the Iran-Iraq wars and some of the conflicts in Lebanon have eased since 1985.

All of these places were what we called "hot spots" in 1985 and now tensions have been lowered. But does Reagan get any credit for that? I ask you what would happen if they were still fighting in those places? Would he be blamed for it? Certainly. So he also should get some of the credit for lowered tensions as well. He convinced Gorbachev that the United States was sincere in wanting those tensions relieved. Gorbachev's ultimate aims, of course, are trade with the United States and a lessening of tensions so that he doesn't have to spend as much on the military as he has been spending. That is the only way he can improve his domestic economy. This being the case, Reagan played to that weakness and extracted the promises.

Now all of these are the accomplishments of a movie idol. Well, he was an idol to some people. Later in his career he admitted he was getting into "B" pictures, and he never did get an Oscar, but nevertheless he was a movie star. Ronald Reagan is a person who studies hard, who does his homework, who knows a lot of what is going on. Remember, as he himself says, ad nauseam, he was on the "rubber chicken" circuit for awhile and had to do his own writing on the speeches he made for General Electric. As a result, he gained quite a bit of knowledge of both national and international affairs. He traveled abroad, not extensively, but quite a bit, and he always took with him some learned person, usually Dick Allen, who became his first national security adviser.

He has an actor's ability to memorize lines and to retain things in his mind. Dick Allen briefed the President quite a bit during their travels, both in Europe and in the Far East. As for domestic issues, he learned a lot by going out and talking to people about what was going on in various sections of the country and about what the problems of the country were. He has such a retentive memory that we used to say, "Never give that guy any kind of misleading facts because sooner or later they are going to come out." Time and time again they did come out, and at the most inopportune moments. He is an avid reader of some offbeat publications—I say offbeat in a nice way, not in a pejorative sense. *Human Events* was one of the magazines he read and remembered. He would read Warren Brookes in *The Washington Times*; Warren Brookes is a good economist and does come up with a lot of good stuff. Reagan would remember what was said in those columns.

The man always did his homework, no matter how much you piled on him at night. He would go up with an arm full of books, and he'd come back the next morning with them all read. Now maybe, like students in some colleges—certainly not this university—he would only skim the material and hope to God nobody quizzed him on it, but nevertheless he did do all his reading. How was he able to accomplish this? The man had a technique of sitting quietly. A lot of people thought he was dumb because he did this. They would say, "The President never spoke up." Why should he? He's got a panel of experts around him. Why not listen? Reagan took from them more than he put in because they knew the subject. He would hear their views, and most of the time they were opposing views. Then he would make up his mind. At meetings where Cabinet officers in discussing an issue were giving him different views on a subject, we would urge him not to commit himself at the table—to wait, look at the position papers afterward, and reach a conclusion once we had summarized the papers for him. Invariably the man had good instincts and judgments. From a conservative point of view, at least, he would come down on the correct side of an issue. To liberals, of course, that may not seem like the right thing to have done.

But Ronald Reagan was first, last, and always a politician. This is where he differed from business executives. When a head of a business corporation makes a decision, that's it: "Don't come back to me again; I don't want to hear this, and I don't want it revisited. Go do it." No second-guessing. And business decisions—at least the ones that I've participated in or have watched—are usually black and white. Politicians never give you a black or white; it's "What shade of gray would you like?" and you can get any color of gray you want from a politician. Now Ronald Reagan, in the end, is a politician. Time and time again he waved his veto pen around, but when the bill was put before him, he signed the thing and didn't veto it.

Look at tax increases under Ronald Reagan. We had a tax cut in 1981 and a tax increase in 1982, 1983, and 1984. We skipped 1985, and we sure as hell got it in 1986. Now there's Ronald Reagan the tax cutter. You are paying more taxes today, by the way, as a percentage of gross national product than at any sustained period in our history. And yet everybody thinks under Ronald Reagan there was a tax cut. Most of the increase, of course, was in Social Security taxes; they are over 15 percent of earned income now. But nevertheless, I give you that as an example of Ronald Reagan. He says he won't raise taxes, but he has to strike a deal. Congress would give him three dollars of cuts for one dollar of tax increase. That's not a bad bargain. He'll take that because it will reduce the deficit. So he signs it.

Due to the relationship between the legislative and the executive branches we have a system in which the budget comes to the President in one piece—take it or leave it. It's unfortunate that this happens. And the way Congress dillydallies, they never get their homework done on time. Rather than have a crisis in government on September 30, on September 29 at 4:30 or maybe even October 1, various appropriations, all in one omnibus bill, will be dumped on the presidential desk at the last moment. Were he not to sign that bill, the government would cease on October 1. That means no tax collectors—which may be a blessing—no customs collectors, no pay for the armed services, and no essential services. A lot of people think there are many in the federal government who are not essential. But it is not a joking matter, when you come right down to it, when you realize the pervasiveness of the federal government and what would happen if the government ground to a halt. So the President, faced with such a situation, signs. Lumped in the one bill are about 20 different items which he said he would not accept under any circumstances. But he has been boxed in by an omnibus bill.

As a politician, Ronald Reagan would rant and rave, but he would sign. So my point is: In the last analysis he is a politician and he would compromise. From appearances, it doesn't look that way, but when you analyze it, that's what happened.

Put it all together, and I'll tell you this. I don't think that a strong-minded, dogmatic individual can make it as president. The American people don't want that. Look at the type of people that the American voter has elected, and look at our candidates in 1988. You don't get that type of person as President of the United States any longer. That era has passed for one reason or another. Maybe it will return, but with all due respect, we will not get an independent-minded man as President of the United States. By this I mean a strong man in the sense that I just talked about: dogmatic, black and white, do it, and that's it. Instead, we will get the politician who will compromise. That, in its essence, is Ronald Reagan.

QUESTION: In the election of a president, what role does the press currently play compared to 20 years ago?

MR. REGAN: I can give my judgment of the press's role in today's elections. I cannot tell you with any degree of authority about 20 years ago. I was there but I was studying other things.

The press plays a dominant role in today's elections. But, the word really shouldn't be "press," it should be "media," and particularly "electronic media." Everything that Bush is doing now, and to which Dukakis is finally wising up, is for a 15-second to hopefully a minute-and-45-second sound bite on the evening news. Whatever scene you see, or whatever you hear the candidates saying, has been plotted by literally dozens of people. You may think I'm exaggerating on this, but I'm not. The next time you take a look at the candidate, forget the candidate and look behind him. Whom do you see? Who are the people? Those who are going to sit there behind him and appear on camera have been carefully arranged. And believe you me, people will kill for that opportunity. Notice the backdrop. If it's a defense speech, you see the hull of a new ship. If it's an educational theme, you see university spires in the distance. If it's to be something on agriculture you see this guy in a white shirt and tie in the middle of a grain field, looking like an odd character. Nevertheless, that is what is planned.

Each day there is a theme. Now maybe this week is farm week. Well, if this is farm week we are going to have to be in Minnesota, or Iowa, or in Nebraska, in Illinois, and maybe Kansas. Each time it is going to be a different scene, but with many similarities. Maybe it's wheat farmers today and the next time it is cotton farmers, or what have you. It's all for the sake of the media. They are trying to impress people.

The speeches are crafted in the same way for the written media. They want to have a couple of sentences that headline writers can use because too many times today you never get the whole text of what the candidate has said. You get a reporter's truncated version of it, but always with the main theme, the headline. Afterwards, as soon as the candidate has finished, people fan out to make particularly sure that the leading writers for AP, UPI, *New York Times, Washington Post, Los Angeles Times*, and *Wall Street Journal* get the right message.

There are conversations daily on the press plane between people who are trying to explain the candidate's views by giving out background papers and the members of the press. You want an example of a botched job of this? Look at the student loan program Dukakis put up the other day. Who here understands it? If anyone here does, he has to be the author because I swear only he could understand it. It certainly didn't come out with any degree of precision, and when pressed, Dukakis's people couldn't explain it. Now this was to be a major theme on education in New Jersey, and they went—of all places—to Kean Community College. Who is the governor of New Jersey? Tom Kean. It's an ancestor of his that that college is named after, and he's a Republican! He's the guy who made one of the major speeches at the Republican Convention. So they went to Kean College for Michael Dukakis.

Next, they have no banners, a bare stage, and he gives this convoluted idea of some type of student loan program where the poor student, the day he graduates, is committed to pay $600 a year back. And that's on an $8,000 dollar loan? Well, who can borrow only $8,000? If a student goes through a college or university today they are usually on the hook for $20-$30,000. So at that point he is going to pay something like $3,000 a year, the year he graduates. Tell me, how can they afford that? But here is Michael Dukakis's new program. Now that is what you *don't* want to do.

Now George Bush? Notice how his image has changed. Why? They got wise and began putting him in a proper framework with clear-cut, concise speeches. That's what they're doing, because everything is played to the media.

QUESTION: Mr. Regan, you invited a question on the deficit. Our former colleague here, Mr. Stein, says it is not all that bad. Is it a problem?

MR. REGAN: Herb Stein is one of the most brilliant economists around, and the fact that he recognizes this confirms my judgment! I've long enjoyed a good relationship with Herb.

Many of us here, like myself, are residents of the Commonwealth of Virginia. We know that Governor Robb did a great job with balancing the budget of the Commonwealth. As a matter of fact for several years we had a surplus under Chuck Robb. Why then is Virginia borrowing money? Any of you own Virginia municipals? Well, if they are balancing the budget, why are they borrowing? The same thing is happening in nearly all 50 states in the Union; most of them are balancing their budgets. But all of them are issuing municipal bonds.

Now you are talking to an old financier and a guy who has participated in the municipal bond market. It is a big market. Why are they doing this? It is called capital budgeting. If you are going to build roads or schools or sewers or bridges, you borrow to build that capital asset. That's why you are issuing bonds, but you are still balancing your budget. Anyone who has ever been in business knows that you borrow to build a building, or to add new stores, or to add new machinery. That's a legitimate, standardized practice, but not for the federal government. You insist that the federal government have a cash budget. Why are you insisting on that? Why do you insist, if we build a new cruiser that costs a billion dollars, that we pay cash for it? Why do you insist, if the federal government builds a building in downtown Richmond, that it pay cash for it? Those of you who are in the real estate business know that's never done. You always put a mortgage on the building or take out a construction loan. You won't permit your federal government to do it, though; you make us run a cash budget.

I'm telling you there is $125 billion annually spent by the federal government for tangible capital assets for which cash is paid. No other government in the world, no other government in the United States, no other corporation has such a cash budget. They have capital budgeting. Now what is our deficit? $146 billion. Well, you can't subtract one from the other; like any good business, or like states, counties, and cities, you have to amortize in order to pay off the bonds. So you have to take a hit for amortization. You come down in the neighborhood of a clear $50 billion of net capital asset buying by the federal government that we call deficit.

Federal deficits in other countries—Japan, Germany, Great Britain, what have you—always go on an entire government basis. The states in Germany have their budget combined with the federal government of Germany for one budget when reporting deficit or surplus. The same thing happens in Japan with the prefectures; the same thing occurs in Great Britain. Not in the United States—the federal budget is in one set of books, the states in another. We just said that states have surpluses. You combine that with the federal and that's another $20 or $30 billion. So, you knock off $80 or $90 billion from that $146 billion and you've got a net operating deficit at the federal level of somewhere in the neighborhood of $50 or $60 billion.

Fifty or sixty billion dollars, my friends, based upon the federal budget of one trillion, isn't that much. And, if you compare it to our gross national product, which is soon to be $5 trillion, it's not even a tenth of one percent. That deficit is not strangling us, and it doesn't have to strangle us if we would merely use standard and common practices. The former secretary of the treasury in the early 1980s who was heard to say "the deficits don't matter" was misquoted. I was saying that during a recession a deficit of this amount can be handled. But when you hear these weird things about $200 billion as far as the eye can see and that we're going into a plastic economy, don't believe it. We are *not* going into any kind of total indebtedness to the rest of the world. We have assets abroad, factories in particular and buildings that are owned by United States entities. They are all considered at cost; they have never been marked to the market. Now if you mark those assets the right way you would find that we own a heck of a lot more abroad than foreigners own here in the United States.

This week the trade deficit is going to be refigured the correct way. Nine years ago, Senator Russell Long [D-La.], in a fit of pique because he couldn't get through some protectionist measures for some of his favorites—and I say this kindly about Russell for he is a shrewd politician and a nice guy, after hours—insisted that the Department of Commerce give its figures on imports with the cost of freight and insurance added to the cost of the imports. But when we figure exports we don't include freight and insurance; it is free alongside ship. Now if that had not been done the deficit monthly would be $1.5-2.5 billion less than it has been. They have finally recognized this and the government will come up with figures without the freight and insurance. Russell wanted the trade deficit to look much worse so that he could get through some protectionist measures.

Now, as for that trade deficit, it is bad, but it is not nearly as bad as has been shown by the initial reports. And when you think about it, a lot of the problem is traced to capital being sent over here. Herb Stein's point is this: What's wrong with that? If the British decide to buy an American company and to run it as an American company, it provides jobs for Americans, it takes raw materials from America and translates them into finished products, and 85-90 percent of the gross of that plant will stay in the United States; maybe 10 percent gets returned to the owners.

Now, in the meantime, no one as yet has turned over the coin. When a Brit comes over here and pays a billion dollars for an American company, or the Japanese, or the Swiss, or the Dutch, what happens to that money? Do we throw it in the Atlantic or bury it in the Mississippi? No, we get cash for that which is plowed back into our economy for additional factories and the like. We've got their money over *here* invested in the United States providing jobs over *here*, providing more capital for the use of our industries. I am not afraid of foreign investment in the United States. You see, I almost get religious on this kind of thing.

QUESTION: Would you give us some of your insights into the operations of the President's staff and his relationship to his staff? From your own experience, what are the differences between being a cabinet member and being close to the President as a staff member?

MR. REGAN: Each president has to set up his staff in accordance with his own preferences. Richard Nixon told me, just prior to my leaving the Office of Chief of Staff, that he wishes he had given Haldeman more authority than he did. Nixon said he tried to run things too much himself. I think that Jimmy Carter probably did the same thing. I don't think Hamilton Jordan had near the authority that I had, for example, as chief of staff. Obviously Eisenhower gave Sherman Adams an awful lot of authority to do things. So the president sets it up the way he wants it.

Ronald Reagan was forced by circumstances into a very peculiar staffing situation in the first administration because he had his very close friend, Ed Meese. I dearly love Ed Meese, but in terms of order and efficiency of running things, he is not the guy to put in charge of a railroad, if you get what I mean. He can think problems through, he can come up with excellent solutions, but he is not a real manager. So Reagan decided not to use him as chief of staff. Instead he chose a guy that he saw was a "take-charge" type of guy who ran an excellent campaign, Jim Baker. Yet he wanted them to be coequal.

Then of course he had the image maker, Mike Deaver. Now Deaver wasn't given that same level; he was just a notch below Baker and Meese. But because Deaver was so close to the president, the situation quickly became, and was called, the triumvirate. The President literally ran things by these three, and it was always difficult for cabinet officers to figure out who was in charge of a particular issue or problem. Should you go to Jim Baker with this problem, or is that Ed Meese's? Mike Deaver and the Cabinet had very little contact, if any. You never knew exactly where you stood.

When I became chief of staff I made the suggestion to Ronald Reagan that it be a single person unless he really wanted others to come in. Ed Meese, by that time, had been nominated to be attorney general and was going through his battle for confirmation. Baker, of course, was out. Deaver, I think, had quietly told the family already that he was going to leave, so the President was aware of that. So I replaced all three. Well, that quickly became apparent in the minds of the press: Here is one replacing three.

That's where I got this sobriquet of "prime minister" and all that type of stuff.

Whoever the next president may be, my recommendation to him is to have a single chief of staff and have everybody report through him to the president, including the national security adviser. That was the Achilles' heel of the second administration. The national security apparatus was outside the loop. It was reporting directly to the President, but no one was really looking closely at it because the President obviously didn't have time to. When the national security advisers—and I say that in the plural because both Robert McFarlane and John Poindexter let the President down, in my judgment—weren't following through on their job, there was nobody supervising them. Now, were they reporting to the chief of staff (my staff or Howard Baker's staff), we might have been able to keep a better eye on that national security apparatus, which I think it needs.

The next president will have to choose his own method of setting up that staff. Everybody doesn't have to be a full assistant to the president, but these are the perks of office, the titles, and people are very jealous as to who is full assistant, or a deputy assistant, or an assistant to a deputy, or what have you. But I wouldn't make everybody, particularly at the start, a full general.

QUESTION: Why is the NSC outside in the Reagan administration?

MR. REGAN: The NSC was set up so the president could have a national security council whose executive director was the national security adviser to the president. Curiously, in the first year of the Reagan administration, the President had Dick Allen report to him through Ed Meese. Allen was used to reporting to the President through Meese, particularly during the campaign, so that relationship was an easy one to continue.

When Bill Clark came along it was different. Clark had been Reagan's chief of staff in Sacramento, and he wasn't about to report to Ed Meese. So they split it off as Carter had done. Brzezinski never reported through Hamilton Jordan, and certainly Kissinger never reported through Haldeman. It was just never done.

QUESTION: I believe Marty Feldstein once submitted an important financial report to you, which you tended to dismiss. What was it about that report you found unsatisfactory?

MR. REGAN: The whole thing except for the preface.

COMMENT: I just thought it was puzzling.

MR. REGAN: Puzzling? All you have to do is read the damn thing. Go back and read it; the man is advocating tax increases to cut down this deficit. This is a brilliant man, head of the Bureau of Economic Research, who can teach economics at Harvard. I could only take undergraduate courses in that. But this guy never understood accounting and didn't understand what I've just said about deficits. Yet as we were coming out of a recession he wanted to raise taxes. Even Keynes wouldn't have done that, let alone this administration, which was supposed to have stood for supply-side economics. The guy never got it straight as to what his priorities were. Was he working for the President, or the President working for him?

Poor Marty—he wanted to bring Cambridge to Washington and the Reagan administration, and it just didn't work. You can't do that sort of thing, and yet he wrote his annual economic report. He submitted it to no one—no one saw the darn thing in advance. All we saw was the preface that we had written for the President to sign, and the rest of the economic report is signed by the three members of the Council of Economic Advisers. So when I went to testify to Congress under oath, I told the truth: I didn't like it. I told the Congress that.

COMMENT: I think the quote was, "You can keep the first seven pages and throw the rest away."

QUESTION: Isn't it a curious thing that under our system of government we have the Federal Reserve? We have an independent agency which, by fixing interests and changing them, can strongly influence political elections. Yet it can't be reached by the President, or, as a political matter, even by Congress.

MR. REGAN: It is the only one of its kind in the world. The head of the Bank of England reports to and is part of the Chancellor of the Exchequer. The head of the Central Bank of Germany fights for his independence, but when push comes to shove he is under the minister of finance. The Bank of Japan is a creature of the government. The Bank of France is wholly under the domination of the minister of finance, and they don't intervene, they don't change interest rates, without consultation with the minister of finance.

Now I will say that, by and large, central banks try not to play politics too much with interest rates during election times. But on the other hand I remind you that the same party has won year after year in Japan, Margaret Thatcher has been able to survive for quite an unusual length of time, and Chancellor Kohl has stayed in for quite a while. So while they claim they don't use politics in setting interest rates, it is there.

Our theory, of course, is that there has to be somebody to protect against the ruination that would come about from letting the executive branch of government handle monetary affairs. It is as though the treasury secretary is such a political figure and a dunderhead that he wouldn't understand monetary controls. It is as though the Congress just didn't trust the executive branch of government. They had to have an independent agency do these things.

There are two levers on our economy: One is fiscal and the other is monetary. Of the two I think the more powerful is monetary. The encouragement of the economy or the braking of the economy is strictly in the hands of the Federal Reserve. And Paul Volcker was a master at smoke and mirrors. The Congress had no idea what he was talking about, but they idolized him. Why? Because he was always against what the administration wanted. He rambled on about these deficits and ruminated as to how things could have been as he literally blew smoke from those cheap cigars into the surrounding atmosphere. He is a nice guy, he tried his best, and he did a good job by and large, but I don't think the Fed should have that independence.

QUESTION: How do you rate the President's style in influencing and coping with a hostile Congress?

MR. REGAN: I'd give him a "B" on that. Ronald Reagan had a love-hate relationship with the Congress. When he first came in he used to tell stories about how well he could get along with a hostile legislature in Sacramento, and how by and large they could reach agreements. But the two Irish descendants—O'Neill and Reagan—were hammer and anvil. Every time they met there were sparks. O'Neill was a dedicated Democratic liberal, with the Irish-American Boston background. He had been brought up in that school. He was devoted to it, he was devoted to the Kennedys, and he could see no good in Ronald Reagan and, as he called it, "his Hollywood glitzy crowd." Therefore, anything that Reagan wanted, O'Neill was opposed to. You had to start from that: there was going to be a battle.

O'Neill never forgave Reagan for the fact that Reagan won the two big battles of 1981: the battle of the budget in which Stockman was able to get budget cuts through the Congress, particularly in social programs, and that Reagan was able to get "five-ten-ten" and other tax cuts through the Congress. O'Neill thought both of those things were wrong. Now from that their relationship deteriorated, and you just never could get them together.

With Bob Dole, the President got along reasonably well, allowing for the dour nature of Bob Dole. But Dole did try to get the President's legislation through. When we had a Republican Senate, it was a lot easier for the administration to do business.

With Robert Byrd, it has been more difficult. Again, it was partisan; it was politics. The Democrats knew 1988 was coming up. There was no desire to give Ronald Reagan much of what he wanted. In fact, Bob Byrd thought that a lot of the Reagan proposals were harmful from an economic point of view as well from as a social point of view. Therefore Reagan had to use stratagems to get things through.

What happened, though, was that the Congress got itself into such economic straits that they had to pass Gramm-Rudman. That law has turned out to be surprisingly strong and a surprisingly good influence on the budget procedure. So Reagan got a prize that I don't think he had really been anticipating. On balance Reagan got probably 70-75 percent of what he wanted, which I would consider to be a gentleman's "B."

NARRATOR: What advice would you give to a businessman going to Washington? It is striking that two presidents, separated by time, brought a number of advisers into government from Wall Street: Franklin Delano Roosevelt and Ronald Reagan. What is the experience from those two periods that other businessmen ought to know about?

MR. REGAN: The Wall Streeters who went with FDR got a lot more sympathetic treatment from the media than those who went with Ronald Reagan. Washington, unlike New York, is a harsh town if you don't go along to get along. If you try to buck the system you will find that you quickly run afoul of the press, and once you have done that, your reputation, once and for all, is established. My reputation is that of a hard, domineering, irritable type of person. The few who know me, including my grandchildren, deny that. But nevertheless, that is the impression that the press will give, and once you are tagged with that you can seldom get away from it. If you are tagged as energetic, you are always energetic, no matter if you are the laziest person in the world. If you get tagged as a guy who does nothing, then you're a nothing guy from then on, no matter what you do.

The businessman is not prepared for that because a businessman comes up in a cocoon. He is protected. He is surrounded by press agents and by officers in his own corporation who work on his image. He seldom gets into shouting matches, except perhaps at an annual meeting or something of that nature. He is never in a confrontational state of mind.

When you go to Washington, the first thing you have to do is reveal all of your assets. Now there are few people in the world who want to reveal all of their assets, so to get around that you put them into a blind trust. There is only one way I can describe that to you so that you can empathize with what happened to me. It's like having a daughter, marrying her off to a guy you have never seen or know nothing about, and hoping for the best. You work, you amass a fortune, and then you take this fortune and give it to a blind trust, never to look at it again. I never knew what the total of my assets were, what my income was, how those assets were invested, or whether indeed they ever existed. When it came time for my income tax, my lawyer would put the form in front of me, put a pad over it, and say, "Sign here, Don." If I saw my income tax return, obviously I could see the gains or losses on it, or know something of what the trustees were doing, or know the size of my income. But you are completely blind. There aren't many businessmen who are willing to do that and put aside all of their assets. Bill Simon told me he lost seven million dollars while he was in Washington as the energy czar and then as secretary of the treasury.

I'll tell you one funny story that happened to me. To some people this may sound like I'm being outrageous, but nevertheless it happened. About the second week I was there in Treasury, my secretary came in and she handed me a check. I looked at the amount on it and said, "What's this?" She said, "That's your pay." I said, "What? That's more like a tip." In those days we were paid $69,000 to be secretary of the treasury; $69,000 to be in charge of the world's greatest money machine. Today we are very munificent—Cabinet officers are paid $99,000. You work for low pay, you put all your assets aside, you are taken out of your cocoon, and now you are exposed.

The first exposure is to the Congress when you have to go up and be confirmed. There, every single item that you ever thought of is examined in one way or another by a committee. My committee happened to be the Finance Committee, and there were many people on the Finance Committee that were hostile to not only the administration, but hostile to Wall Street. As a prominent Wall Streeter, I was hit right off the bat with when-did-you-stop-beating-your-wife type of questions. You have to sit there in the glare of the lights testifying and hoping to God that you don't put your foot in your mouth the first time out of the box. But you have to go through that lengthy procedure.

Then you are surrounded by the press, who immediately pick up where the senators have left off to ask all of the trivial questions that accompany those larger questions. Now somewhere along the line you have made a misstatement, or you have somehow given the wrong impression. You will find *that* in the headlines, and no one hears about all the rest that you said. By the time you get through you have been put through the wringer.

The businessman going to Washington has got to be prepared for this. There is an old line from Harry Truman: "If you can't stand the heat, stay out of the kitchen." On the other hand, I think that's a shame. Many businessmen have told me they wouldn't have gone through what I went through for anything. "Why did you bother to do it?" they ask. Well, call it an attack of patriotism, or blindness, or what have you.

But how many people could say "no" after having the following experience? I was sitting in my home in New Jersey with my wife. It was just after the seven o'clock news had started. I was having a glass of white wine, which I usually do, when the phone rang. My wife answered it, turned to me, and said, "It's from Ronald Reagan." Now this was 3 or 4 December 1980, about a month after the election. I had a little warning that he might be calling me because a friend had been telling me that I was on the original list for secretary of the treasury. It had been cut down and so forth, but I was still on it.

When I answered the phone—I answer very abruptly—I said, "Hello, Regan," and this voice said, "Well, I guess I'm going to have to get used to that pronunciation of that name." So I said, "Good evening, Mr. President," and offered him congratulations as it was the first time I had talked to him since the election: "Congratulations and best wishes in Washington." He said, "Well, that's what I'm calling about. I want you to be my secretary of the treasury." I said yes, and he said, "What? Don't you want to think it over or talk it over?" I said, "What's to think over? What's to talk over?" Who can say to a new incoming president, "No, Mr. President, stuff that job; I can't take Washington and the heat; I'm just not going to do it"? So I said, "Yes."

I say that businessmen should say yes. I also say businessmen should be prepared to take the heat, because if they aren't, what they get from government they deserve. They have no excuse in their locker room, in the lunchroom, or anywhere else, to condemn the federal government if they've had an opportunity to serve and didn't take it.

NARRATOR: It's a very good point on which to end. Thank you very much.

CHAPTER 4

REAGAN: THE PERSON AND THE POLITICAL LEADER

LYN NOFZIGER

NARRATOR: Lyn Nofziger is the veteran in Ronald Reagan's campaigns, going back to 1966. He graduated from San Jose College and spent 16 years as a reporter for the Copley newspapers, the last eight years of that period in Washington. He covered the 1960 and 1964 presidential campaigns. His association with President Reagan began through his brother, Neal—or as he calls him, "Moon" Reagan—who worked as TV adviser in the Goldwater campaign.

After Reagan's campaign for the governor's office, Mr. Nofziger was asked to stay on. He spent nearly two years in the first term as communications director. He then left the statehouse to become a deputy assistant to President Nixon for congressional relations. He served next as deputy chairman for communications of the Republican National Committee, and after that as director of Nixon's Reelection Campaign Committee in California. In 1973–75 he set up his own political consulting business. He returned to Reagan's camp with the campaign of 1976 and Ronald Reagan's entrance into national politics.

With the funds left over from that campaign he established and managed a political action committee called Citizens for the Republic. In March 1979 he joined Reagan's successful campaign for the presidency. Then because of the well-publicized difference with John Sears, he departed the campaign, only to return in June of 1980 as press secretary and then as assistant to President Reagan for political affairs. He served in the White House for about a year,

69

even though he had expressed his desire to go back to California after the campaign. Since then he has had his own political consulting firm. Throughout his career, he has maintained contacts with good friends such as Ed Meese and Bill Clark, and his involvement in California and national politics offers a continuity in his career that practically no other political figure has had. We are delighted to have you with us.

MR. NOFZIGER: Thank you very much. I thought that instead of trying to talk to you about Reagan policies and programs I would talk to you about Ronald Reagan as a person. The reason for this is that (1) you can read about policies pretty thoroughly in the papers, and (2) there are others much more qualified to discuss them than myself. Some of these people have been with Reagan for longer segments of the eight years, and have been more directly involved in policy matters.

I thought talking about Reagan, the man, might give some insight into why he was the kind of president he was. I really do have a special perspective on Ronald Reagan. I have known him over the whole span of his political career, and that's not true of very many people, with the exception of Nancy. Even those who started out with him when he first entered the governor's office did not have the advantage of having watched him become governor. I was fortunate enough to spend almost a year in that first gubernatorial campaign where I watched him learn and develop as a politician.

I have known Ronald Reagan since 1965. I might as well confess and tell you that the first time I met him I wasn't sober—reporters being what they are. In June 1965 in Ohio there was a series of eight dinners called a "Salute to Ray Bliss," who at the time was the Ohio state chairman and later became the national Republican chairman and a very well known and competent working politician. Dwight D. Eisenhower was scheduled to make the major speech in Cleveland. I was going out to Cleveland to cover the speech. I had heard that Ronald Reagan, who had become very famous as something besides an actor due to the speech he made in the 1964 campaign, was coming to Ohio to speak at the dinner in Cincinnati. The day before that he was going to a little town called Newark, Ohio, to do a fund raiser for John Ashbrook, the conservative congressman. They were having a reception for him at some wealthy person's farm and I was invited. I wanted to meet Ronald Reagan to see what he was like informally.

In those days Ronald Reagan was not flying. He had flown before the war but after the war decided that the odds were against him. (After airplanes were made safe, he figured the odds were against him.) So he didn't fly again, I would suspect, from 1945 until he ran for governor in 1966. We told him that if he was going to campaign in California he would have to fly; the state is just too big. So he did, but he wouldn't fly in anything less than a two-engine plane. For several years after he began flying, he and Nancy would fly separately because they figured that if the airplane crashed one of them would have to live to take care of the kids. I used to say, "Take the kids with you and then it doesn't matter." That didn't seem to get me anywhere either.

Reagan had come into Newark, Ohio, on a train and was therefore late. He arrived at the cocktail party just as everybody was leaving to go hear him speak. When I introduced myself to him, he kind of looked down his nose at me and I'm sure he thought, "What is this drunken reporter doing here?" That, however, is the first time I met Ronald Reagan. I covered his speech, and when I got up the next morning to write my story, I couldn't read my notes. Fortunately by this time I was a senior reporter with Copley and could get away with things like that.

The next time I met Reagan was on another rather auspicious occasion. It was the day the Watts riots broke out in 1965. I had to go to California for a meeting in San Diego with our publishers, so I called Moon Reagan and said, "Moon, I'm coming out to California. I know your brother is going to run for governor [even though he was denying it] and I'd like to interview him." Moon set up a lunch for us at the Brown Derby in Hollywood. Reagan as usual was late—about 20 minutes late. He came in and I got up and introduced myself. I said, "You probably don't remember, but we've met before," and he said, "Oh, yes I do." I dropped that subject very quickly.

As usual, and this is an interesting thing about Ronald Reagan, he was very coy about saying whether or not he would run. It was clear to me that he would, however. He had a financial money-raising team put together, some very wealthy Republicans. He had been going up and down the state making speeches. The talk in all of the papers was that he was going to run. He would not say that he would run; he said that he might or might not, he was thinking about it. Actually he didn't announce that he was going to run until January 1966. So there was a period there of well over six months when everybody but Ronald Reagan knew that he was going to run. That is typical of him, however. He always gives himself a chance to back out if it looks as if it is not going to be the right thing to do. He has a very good feeling for what is right for Ronald Reagan and what is not right. He has a very good political sense.

In December 1966—and this is something that you won't read in most books because most people don't know about it—several of us met in Reagan's house in Pacific Palisades. We sat down and said, "OK, you've been elected governor now." He hadn't even been sworn in yet. "Let's look and see what we can do about electing you president in 1968." Once again, there were three or four of his very wealthy supporters there and three or four of us who were politicians. Out of that meeting the moneyed people found the money to hire a man named F. Clifton White, whom some of you may know. He is the man who drafted Barry Goldwater in 1963. White was hired to begin looking around the country to see whether or not Ronald Reagan should run for president.

By early 1968, Tom Reed, who later became secretary of the Air Force in the Ford administration, and myself became the prime movers behind Reagan's run for the presidency. He was very reluctant—and I think this time genuinely so—but we got him to agree to be a favorite son candidate. That's the way you control the delegation in California. The awarding of delegates in California is not proportional. There, you win the presidential primary and control all the members of the delegation. As governor, he clearly should have controlled the delegation, and the way to accomplish that was to run him as a favorite son. He was very reluctant to become a candidate, however, and in retrospect he was absolutely right. He felt that he had not even been governor for two years and that all of a sudden wanting to be president was presumptuous.

Tom Reed and I both felt that we should run him before he had any political scars. We figured that if he didn't run, a Republican would probably win anyway. Eight years later Ronald Reagan would be a kind of old hack politician, and besides that he would be an old man. So we pushed and pushed, while he did almost nothing to help us. After we got to the convention in Miami Beach and he had actually talked to delegates, he was interested in making a serious run at it. Then we said, "Well, the only way you can do that is to announce that you are no longer a favorite son, that you are a bona fide candidate."

Actually Bill Knowland, the former United States senator, is the guy who came up with that idea, but Reagan accepted it, and the day before they actually balloted at the convention, he announced he was a full-fledged candidate for president, but it was much too late. We had hoped that if we could keep Nixon from winning on the first ballot, the delegates that were no longer committed to Nixon would create a slide toward Reagan. Both the Nixon and Rockefeller people recognized this, but while Nelson Rockefeller knew how to win New York, he had no idea how to win the presidency. He had politicians around him who couldn't count delegates. That's a fatal flaw if you are trying to get someone elected president. They thought they had enough delegates that, between themselves and us, we could stop Nixon. We knew that there weren't enough, but we couldn't convince them, so a couple of steps that might have been taken weren't, and Reagan was not nominated there in 1968: Nixon was.

Reagan said to me afterward, and this speaks well for him, "I don't feel badly about this. I was not ready." I think that's interesting. He recognized that he did not have enough experience in governing to be comfortable as president. The thing to always remember about presidents is that you never know whether they are going to be good until they get into the White House. There are presidents, such as Harding, who everyone thinks will be great before they are elected, but you have to wait and see how a person acts under various kinds of pressures. I don't think that the man himself knows how he is going to react until he gets in there.

Reagan, incidentally, was certainly a different kind of president, but he was also a different kind of governor. He was the same kind of governor as he was president. He was a man who didn't really take himself all that seriously. So many men who are elected governor or president think that they were anointed by the Lord to serve and therefore should not be questioned. They know everything there is to know, and one should not argue with them. That was not the case with Reagan; he never took himself too seriously and never thought that the job was one that a man ought to work at 18 or 20 hours a day. He did not do that. I think he instinctively knew—I happen to agree with this—that the job of the president, and to a little lesser extent the job of governor, is not to micromanage the government.

Jimmy Carter's main flaw was that he could see every tree but he had trouble seeing the forest. He worried about minor things. When he first took office, he was keeping the schedule of who played tennis on the White House tennis courts. He was worrying about who his senior staff people hired as their secretaries. Well, no president should worry about that. That's not his job, and Reagan understood that. Maybe he understood it a little too well. He always looked at the job this way: A president should be the man who sets the policy, who lays out the philosophy of government, who says what direction to go in, and who was there to make the tough and major decisions. He did that. He had a knack for making a tough decision and never looking back.

Shortly after Reagan became governor, there was a cop killer who was up for execution. The law had just been changed again to allow executions, so nobody had been executed in California for about seven years. Pat Brown executed one man and found the situation too harrowing to ever execute anybody else. He kept postponing the execution. Reagan was tortured by the decision. He prayed—he is a devout Christian—talked to his minister, talked to others, and then went ahead and let an execution go forward. He never really looked back. There were never any "what if's", at least publicly. He made the decision and was then able to move on. Incidentally, he never had another person executed. For a person of some sensitivity, which he is, it must have been a very difficult decision to make. I had no trouble with it, but I didn't have to make the decision.

Reagan is a man who has a great feeling for the people around him. I'd like to illustrate that. Here is a man whom much of the press has described as cold-hearted and uncaring, yet he does care about people. When he first became governor, we all went in to run the state and thought that we were very important people. We worked long hours. Reagan, being a smart man, would close up his office about 5:00 or 5:30 p.m. and go home. He came in about 8:30 or 9:00 a.m. Once in a while we could get him up early to have a 7:30 breakfast, but as a rule you shouldn't do that with Reagan. He's no good in the morning at all. He's no good late at night either. He's a man who will tell you bluntly, "Listen, I need eight hours sleep, and I do better on nine." I used to tell people that he was half a disciple of Benjamin Franklin; he believes in early to bed. The press would comment on this terrible man who was going home early while the state was falling apart, but Reagan would take his reading home, put on his pajamas and sit there and read. In between he might watch television.

He did not expect the people who were working for him to put in those long hours either. The California governor's office is built in a square around a patio. The governor's own office is in one corner, and the offices of his senior staff are around the quadrangle. He would come walking down the corridor and stick his head into offices where there would be a meeting going on or something, and say, "Gee, fellows, it's time to go home. Go home to your wife and kids." Being very important people, we would ask, "Well, who is going to get all the work done?" He said on more than one occasion, and he was absolutely right, "Look, it doesn't matter. Most of it doesn't matter whether you get it done or not." He was absolutely right. The problem with this country is not that we don't have good government; it's that we have too much government. Reagan instinctively understood that.

He was also worried about the effect that the job would have on people's families. I've known an awful lot of people who have had marriage problems and gotten divorces because they spent too much time in their government offices. They became too close to their government secretaries and didn't go home soon enough.

I have a personal example that I'd like to share with you about the kind of caring man Reagan is. During the campaign of 1966, we had come into Los Angeles International Airport and were going to have a press conference there. My wife and two daughters—we were still living in Virginia—had come out to California for the summer and came down to the airport to meet me. They hadn't seen very much of me for the last six or seven months. We came in and I said to them, "Now we have business here. If you will just stand to one side, I'll talk to you after we're through." So we went ahead and held our press conference. Afterwards, I picked them up and we went home. I didn't think anything more about it.

A few days later we were up at Lake Tahoe having a brainstorming session in a big fancy cabin, which had a large veranda overlooking the lake. Three or four of us were outside having a drink before dinner, and Reagan wandered out and said, "Lyn, I want to talk to you." He took me over on the side and said,

"Lyn, you've got to be nicer to your wife and children." I said, "What in the hell are you talking about?" "Well," he said, "the other day when we came into Los Angeles you were pretty rude to them." Now the candidate should not have been paying any attention to this; he should have been worrying about his press conference. Anyway, I said, "Look, it was all right; they understood." He said, "Take it from an old married man. You've got to be nicer to your wife and children." I said, "Hey, I've been married longer than you," and he said, "Not if you count both of my wives." So he is a caring man.

Talking about both his wives, perhaps the single thing in Ronald Reagan's life that affected him most was his divorce from Jane Wyman. He didn't want it. She walked away from him basically on the grounds that he was boring, which is interesting. Clearly she wasn't interested in politics. He had always been interested in politics, even though he had been a Democrat. He had been active in the Screen Actors Guild and for five or six years had been the president of it. He was interested in these kinds of things. She apparently was interested in the social life of Hollywood, so she divorced him. It left him with a very empty feeling, with a feeling that it should not have happened. He was raised in a somewhat puritan family. His father had been an alcoholic and a Catholic, but his mother was a member of the Disciples of Christ. She was very devout. The boys had been raised in that church. Therefore, he thought divorce was wrong.

When he married Nancy Davis, I am sure that he said to himself, "Nothing is ever going to destroy this marriage." Nancy is not the easiest lady in the world to live with. I've never lived with her, but I've been around her. Anybody who has been around Ronald Reagan will tell you that he has always walked that extra mile to make sure that their marriage stayed together. The part of his life that had to do with Jane Wyman is something that he has tried to put to one side. He has taken hold of his life with Nancy to make sure that his belief in marriage was right. If you read his autobiography, *Where's the Rest of Me?*, written in 1965, you will find that he dispenses with his first marriage in about two paragraphs. That's incredible, but it's just the way he is.

One of the things that most people who have been close to Ronald Reagan notice is that there is a veil between Ronald Reagan and the rest of the world. You never really feel that you have gotten inside the guy, even if you know him well. I traveled with him pretty much alone every day for nearly nine months, and we'd sit in back of the car or on the plane together. You get to know somebody pretty well under these circumstances; but I always felt there was something there separating Ronald Reagan from the rest of the world. I don't know whether Nancy feels it, but I don't know anyone else who doesn't. I don't know if it is a protective mechanism due to something that happened to him as a poor boy. It might be due to the fact that as a movie actor you are harried by people who want autographs and want to get next to you. Maybe he was protecting himself from that. Maybe he decided after Jane Wyman that he was never going to let anything hurt him again. Whatever the cause, there is a veil there.

I'd like to read a letter that a friend of mine who knows Ronald Reagan really well wrote me. It reflects my own frustration with Reagan. It reads, "Which is the real Ronald Reagan, the benign flesh and blood man next to us in the plane seat, or the disembodied, searching spirit hovering out there in air too thin for us to breathe?" After he had been talking about Ronald Reagan's achievements, he went on to say, "The most puzzling irony of all is that these achievements have left him cool, unvain, incurious, and as private as a Trappist monk." Nancy says, "What you see is what you get." I used to say that too, but it isn't that simple, believe me, and she knows it isn't. He is a very private man. It's very hard to find out just what is going on in that mind of his.

Reagan, however, is a lot more than just cool, unvain, and incurious. That's not quite true. In some ways he is incurious. But he is an omnivorous reader, and if you are an omnivorous reader, you can't be entirely incurious. I think that what my friend was driving at is that his curiosity is not about what is going on today, but a general curiosity that we all have. As I say, he has to be more than a kind of distant critter because too many people love him. You don't love somebody who is distant from you. I love him, and the people who have worked for him over the years love him. People who, before they had known him, did not like him, or hated him, or who were contemptuous of him, came to know him and then to respect him. More than that, they came to love him.

I think if you spoke to Ed Meese or Bill Clark or Kathy Osborne, who is his personal secretary, or to literally hundreds of people who have come to know him in a rather close and intimate way, they will tell you that they love Ronald Reagan. Howard Baker, who became Ronald Reagan's chief of staff by accident, is a nice man, but Reagan hated him because of the Panama Canal. He thought that Baker was lightweight, and Howard Baker thought much the same about Ronald Reagan. He thought that Reagan was a lightweight who didn't know much. At the insistence of Paul Laxalt, however, Baker became Reagan's chief of staff and eventually became very much a fan of Ronald Reagan. The same was true of Margaret Heckler, the congresswoman who lost to Barney Frank and later became Ronald Reagan's secretary of HHS (Health and Human Services). She will tell you the same thing: "I love Ronald Reagan." So there is much more to him than there appears to be from a distance.

Often a politician can stir the masses but be no good at all in dealing with individuals. On the other hand, he might be very good with individuals, but have trouble relating to people as a whole. But Reagan is unique because he appeals to people in both ways.

I keep going back to the campaign of 1966 because it was then that I really got to know him. Also, Ronald Reagan has not changed over the years. It is an amazing thing to me. So many people enter politics, get elected to the state legislature, and get a little bit of ego; they get elected to the state Senate and there's a little more ego; and then they get to be a United States representative and they think they are pretty important. Finally, they wind up as a governor or a United States senator or a presidential candidate, and by this time they think the Lord has anointed them. Reagan has never gotten that way. He is today the same nice man that he was 25 years ago. It is really incredible. You can still talk with him, you can still argue with him, and you can still sit down and tell jokes with him.

Once in a while when Reagan was President, a call would come from the White House and someone would say, "Mr. Nofziger, the President wants to talk to you." Everybody would hear this sotto voce and think, "My God, Nofziger is being consulted on matters of state." Usually, however, it was just that the President had run into a joke that he thought I'd like. He's found me in Colorado, California, and just about anywhere else that I might be just to tell me a joke. He didn't need my advice when I was out in the country. He did very well by himself. He is a nice man and a caring man; he is a moral man.

I've been blessed by Ronald Reagan because he is one of not very many candidates who, when you put him to bed, stays in bed. He's not out chasing; he's not much of a drinker. I've never seen him take more than a couple of drinks, so you don't have to worry about him getting drunk. If he misspeaks, it is because he is cold sober. He probably would have been better off with a couple of drinks.

I remember a funny story about Reagan's drinking. We were on an airplane one day and there were some press traveling with us, including one reporter that Reagan didn't like at all. He thought the man had lied about him in one thing or another, which is probably true. So we were sitting in our seats with this reporter and a couple of others across the aisle. The stewardess came down the aisle and asked us if we would like a drink. Reagan said to me, "I'd really like a split of champagne, but if I have one, that s.o.b. across the aisle is going to write that I'm a heavy drinker." So instead of a split of champagne, he had a diet coke. Then he looked across the aisle and saw that the guy he disliked had ordered a split of champagne. He sat there and cursed him under his breath as if the guy had done it deliberately.

Reagan is a gentleman. He's the kind of person who helps a lady into her chair, opens the door of the car for her. While he can tell a dirty joke as well as anybody, I have never heard him make an off-color remark around a woman. He is a courtly, old-fashioned gentleman. He is the kind of guy that your mother hoped you ladies would marry. That is a little unusual for today's politicians. He is certainly no Lyndon Johnson.

Yet at the same time he is very much a man's man. Men like his company. He is an outdoorsman, as you know; he rides horses. As a poor boy growing up in Illinois he had always wanted to ride horses, but couldn't afford it. So when he grew up and got a job as a radio announcer, he joined the cavalry reserves so he could learn to ride horses. Actually he was a member of the cavalry when World War II came along. Of course, we had no horses in the military by then, so they stuck him in an outfit that was making movies for national morale.

I have another memory, once again from the campaign of 1966. Reagan had a ranch outside of Los Angeles just northwest of the San Fernando Valley in a place called Malibu Canyon. He had a hundred or so acres out there and was raising a few thoroughbreds. He always lost money on thoroughbreds and never raced them; he raised them simply because he enjoyed it. He could afford to lose money on them. He loved to ride and to jump. When he'd go riding, ordinarily he wouldn't wear blue jeans like western cowboys do; he'd put on some jodhpurs and boots and go riding his horse over the jumps. One day a television reporter said, "I would love to come out and do a feature on Ronald Reagan riding on his ranch." So I said, "Fine, this will be really good PR."

Reagan and I went to the ranch to get him ready for this television segment, and he came strolling out of the house in jodhpurs and boots. I looked at him and said, "Where are your jeans?" "Well," he said, "I'm going to ride the horse over the jumps." I said, "Dammit, Ron, you can't do that here. You are in California; you are a Westerner. If the people in this state see you like that they are going to think you are a sissy." When I said, "I suppose you are going to use an Eastern saddle too," he said, "Of course." I told him, "You can't do it." So he very reluctantly and grouchily went back into the house and put on a pair of jeans. Then he threw a Western saddle on his horse, and we got a great bit of publicity. You wouldn't have to tell him that today.

He is very much an outdoorsman; he loves to go up to that ranch of his and chop wood and clear brush. He is a natural athlete. He always said he was not a nut on golf, but he was quite a good golfer. He liked to tell a story relating to his golf game. He was invited to play one day with former President Eisenhower, and the other golfers asked him what his handicap was. He hemmed and hawed and said that he was a lousy golfer. Afterward, however, he said, "You know, it's a terrible thing. I went out and shot one of the best games I've ever shot. I was so embarrassed I didn't know what to do."

He likes to ride, and he likes to work with his hands. He is not a hunter or fisherman, but an outdoorsman. He is in many respects what you would have to call a regular guy; men like him, women like him, and dogs like him. That dogs like him I think means more to him than the fact that men and women like him.

Reagan is the kind of guy you'd like to sit down and have a beer with. I think one of the things that helped elect him was the fact that the average blue-collar guy could relate to him. Ronald Reagan is not a blue-collar man. He grew up poor and delighted in making money. There is a saying, "I've been rich and I've been poor, and rich is better." He makes no bones about it. He doesn't say, "I'm not really well to do and I really don't want all these trappings of power." He loves them. But at the same time he doesn't demand them; he accepts them. As I say, one of the things I'm convinced helps him with the electorate is that the average guy sitting there with his can of beer watching Ronald Reagan feels a kinship with him. Don't ask me why.

Nobody in the whole world uses a television camera for getting to people better than Ronald Reagan. Of course, he has had a lot of experience. He acquired television experience in the days of live television and "GE Theater." One of the things he'll tell you—and this is entirely different from what people used to say—is that you're not looking at a lens on the camera, you are looking through the lens to some guy sitting in his living room. You are talking to that particular person. That person is an individual sitting there, and you are looking right at the lens talking to him. That is what Reagan always did. He used the camera as a means of communicating, not to 20 million people, but to 20 million individuals. He said, "You've got to look them in the eye." I'm not sure I agree with him, but he also says, "The camera does not lie. If you are a phony, you come across as a phony; if you are not, if you are sincere and well-meaning, you come across as sincere and well-meaning."

My old friend Jesse Unruh was, perhaps, the best politician to come along in California history. He was a Democrat and speaker of the State Assembly. He could have been elected to the United States Senate, where I'm convinced he would have made Lyndon Johnson look like a rank amateur, but he wanted to be governor of the state of California. So he ran against Ronald Reagan in 1970, which wasn't very smart because Jess was short and ugly, and short and ugly doesn't come across on television as well as tall and handsome. Being smart wasn't enough. Jess is dead now, but three or four years ago I was out in Palm Springs making a speech. He was also down there making a speech to the same group of people, and after we finished, we had lunch together. He said, "You know, the difference between Reagan and most politicians is that Reagan believes what he says. He can say 'two and two are four,' and he can say 'two and two are six' ten minutes from now, and he absolutely believes two and two are six. I might say two and two are four now and ten minutes later say two and two are six, but everybody knows I'm lying. That is the difference politically between Ronald Reagan and most politicians. Ronald Reagan absolutely believes what he is telling you. He sounds sincere because he is sincere. I'm not going to sound sincere when I tell you two and two are six because I know it isn't true. Ronald Reagan is convinced it is." Ronald Reagan is convinced that this kind of sincerity comes across on television. He didn't make it up; that's just the way he is.

Yet despite all this, sometimes one does feel that Reagan lives in a world of his own. Regarding the guy who was talking about him being off in air too thin for the rest of us to breathe, I suppose that's as good a way as any of putting it. When Reagan is not focused on what he has to do, you do get the feeling that he is off in a world of his own. He won't think about things that he ought to do. Somebody has to come along and remind him. "Hey governor," "Hey Mr. President," or "Hey Ron, so-and-so just died. You ought to call his widow." "Oh, yes, of course," he would reply. He wouldn't think of it by himself. I think one of the reasons is that he is such a private man. He doesn't like to appear to be intruding or interfering in other people's affairs, personal problems, or sorrows, but when he makes the telephone call or writes the letter, nobody does it better. I'd like to hire Ronald Reagan as a professional phone caller, so when somebody I know dies he can call the widow and commiserate with her on my behalf. The letters he writes are beautiful.

After Reagan left the governor's office, the woman who had been his personal secretary all those years, Helene Von Damm, collected a lot of his letters and decided to write a book about Ronald Reagan and the letters he wrote. Helene had no particular background in writing anything, except Ronald Reagan's letters, so I wound up ghosting the book for her. As a result I read hundreds of Ronald Reagan letters, and they are just outstanding. In 1976 we published it in paperback form. It didn't sell very well. It ought to be redone and updated. It contains letters of advice to his children, letters of advice to other people's children, letters of response to critics in which he was always friendly and understanding. He would say to his critics, "Hey, we don't have to get mad at each other even though we differ." He does those things very well, but most of the time somebody has to say, "Ron, you ought to write a letter to so-and-so." Many of the other people and I who have been close to him, if we heard that something has happened to somebody whom Reagan knows or has worked with, would call his secretary and ask, "Hey, did you know that such and such happened?" She would give him the message.

I have personal knowledge of that. My daughter had to go into the hospital on January 20 of this year, which was the last day Reagan was in office. The last telephone call Ronald Reagan made from his office was to Georgetown University Hospital. He was looking for my daughter to cheer her up and so forth. His daughter Maureen had heard about my daughter and told her father. He couldn't find her, by the way. They were looking for Susan Nofziger and unfortunately she was married, so he ended up talking to my wife. Nevertheless, he is a caring man. That's the kind of thing that makes you love Ronald Reagan.

He is, as I say, a nice man. He doesn't usually hold a grudge. He has a terrible time firing people. I think that's probably one of his weaknesses. Another weakness is that he is not very good at hiring people.

I only know of one instance when he personally fired someone and only a couple where he set out on his own to have somebody fired. The rest of the time we had to go to him and say, "Hey, you've got to fire so-and-so." It is something that he doesn't like to do. The only time he fired anybody was on primary day in New Hampshire in 1980. It was one of the great days in my life when he called in John Sears, Jim Lake, and Charlie Black to fire them. I had known since the day before that it was going to happen, and as I say, it was one of the great days of my life.

In another instance, he demanded that a man be fired, over the objections of his campaign management. The man had goofed up badly three or four times, and Reagan began to think it was deliberate. It wasn't deliberate; the guy was just stupid. It was easier, however, for Ronald Reagan to think that he was malicious. I don't know whether that's good or bad.

As for hiring people, most of the people in his administration he didn't hire. One of the things that happened to him, especially as President, was that the people who were hired were not really loyal to Ronald Reagan. That doesn't mean they weren't competent. Many of the people in the White House—and it got worse as time went on—had never worked for Reagan and didn't really agree with him philosophically. This contrasted with his situation as governor, where the people around him, almost without exception, were strong pro-Reagan people who believed the way he did philosophically.

My feeling is that Ronald Reagan was a very good president, but he could have been a better president had he paid more specific attention to who was working for him. His first chief of staff had been George Bush's man; his second chief of staff had been a guy who contributed to the Democratic party in the 1980 campaign, Don Regan; his third chief of staff was Howard Baker, who was obviously more liberal than Reagan and disagreed with him on many things; and his last chief of staff was Ken Duberstein, who is a very nice fellow but came out of Jack Javits' Senate office as a much more liberal Republican. It is very difficult when a man with a strong ideology and philosophy of government like Reagan brings in people who don't agree with his philosophy of government. It means you are not going to get as much done as you might have otherwise.

The whole personnel thing is something that makes him uncomfortable. Ronald Reagan never once hired me and never once fired me. Although there are reporters who will tell you he has fired me three or four times, I maintain that I quit. I keep saying, "Listen, if I'd been fired, I wouldn't have been dumb enough to go back and ask for more."

When he was elected President, he had to hire people, but some people around him were recommended. When he hired Jim Baker as his chief of staff, he hardly knew Jim Baker. Baker had impressed Nancy, Mike Deaver, and Stu Spencer, who had run Reagan's campaigns in California in 1966 and 1970 and was close to Baker.

One of the few people that he personally hired for his Cabinet he could never brag about because another guy claimed responsibility for it. There is a funny little story behind this. Bill Clements, the governor of Texas, came out to see Reagan up at Pacific Palisades. It was probably in late November of 1980. We always tried to have somebody with Reagan when he was with one of these politicians because we never quite trusted Reagan. He's a nice man and sometimes apt to give away the store. I was up at the house with Reagan when Bill Clements came in. He talked about a number of things before finally coming to his point. He had come to recommend Cap Weinberger for secretary of defense. He had worked in the Nixon administration as deputy secretary of defense when Cap was secretary of HHS, head of the Federal Trade Commission, and head of the Office of Management and Budget. So Clements knew Cap and liked him, but just as importantly he didn't like John Tower, who also wanted to be secretary of defense. Reagan was very noncommittal, but listened. When Bill Clements had gone, Reagan turned to me and said, "You know, I didn't want to tell him this, but it had already occurred to me to name Cap Weinberger secretary of defense. I didn't want to tell him. He would think that I had stolen his idea." So he went ahead and named Cap Weinberger secretary of defense and to this day, as far as I know, Bill Clements thinks it was his idea.

Most of the people who joined the administration either asked for their jobs, such as Bill Smith, or were recommended. Many were not close to Reagan at all. He did not have a list of people whom he was going to hire. He didn't even have a list of the Carter people he was going to fire. This turned out to be one of my jobs at the White House, and I had a hard time getting rid of some Carter people. It was a job I enjoyed immensely, but it wasn't a job that Reagan really cared anything about. He has this funny problem. He's too trusting. He thinks that if you work for him you'll like him and be loyal to him. He's right about 90 percent of the time, but unfortunately the other 10 percent can create problems.

He is a man with good political instincts. He knows when he ought to announce that he is running for office. I am a hawk in these things; I want a guy in there early so he can begin to raise money and put things together. Reagan, who does nothing but win, was too dumb to listen to me. We began putting the 1966 campaign together in July 1965, but we couldn't get him to announce until late November 1965.

We began to put the 1980 presidential campaign together in March 1979; we couldn't get him to announce until late November 1979. He will wait until a time when he feels he is comfortable, and to heck with all of you politicians who think you know what you are doing. He is a guy who will make those major decisions. In 1966 Stu Spencer and Bill Roberts were running his campaign. They are very good professional politicians, two of the best political operatives I have ever known. They were leery of Reagan when they ran him for governor. They'd been hired to do it, but they thought that Reagan was not very smart. They thought that he was inexperienced in politics, which he was. So they wanted to put tight controls on him.

The stories that were running in the papers were indeed that he was a controlled candidate, that he memorized his answers and his speeches, and that it would be a total disaster if he was left on his own. Well, Bill and Stu thought that they could handle this image problem, and Reagan felt very strongly that they couldn't. Over their objections he said, "I'm going to start taking questions." Remember, this was in 1966 when we were reaching the height of problems in Vietnam. There were problems on the campuses, especially in California. There was a lot of turmoil in the state and in the country. Here was this actor thinking that he could be governor of California, and he decided, "I have to prove to these people that I am more than an actor." He was right, and he did it. Everywhere he went he took questions. He did his homework, answered those questions, and made very few mistakes. I think that is one of the reasons why he won so handily.

I felt all along he would win. I had been out with him two or three times. I came back one time and said to Bill Roberts, "You know, there is something between Ronald Reagan and the people. I can't put a handle on it, but there is something there. He is going to be elected. You know, if he is elected governor, he could even be president one day." I like to brag about this, but the funniest thing is that Bill Roberts turned to me and said, "Oh, Lyn, what will that poor soul do if he ever gets elected governor?" So although there was not a lot of confidence in Ronald Reagan at that time, I was naive enough to think that there was something there.

The decision to debate in 1980 was one Reagan made by himself. I got up one morning in Sioux Falls, South Dakota, and said to myself, "We are going to have to debate. This campaign is just flat, and we have to do something to get moving." (I had been opposed to the idea of debates.) So I went to see Stu Spencer who was packing. He looked up from his suitcase and said, "You know, Lyn, we are going to have to debate." I said, "You s.o.b., I came down here to tell you that." That same day just by chance I rode out to the airplane with Ronald Reagan. We were sitting there talking and he said, "You know, Lyn, we are going to have to debate." I said, "Damn you. When we get to the airplane and you say that we have to debate, they are going to think that I talked you into it. They are all going to be mad at me." So when I got on the airplane I went to Stu and said, "Hey, Reagan decided this on his own." Although we might have won anyway, Reagan instinctively understood that things were not moving and that something had to be done. That was good political instinct.

In 1976 he had lost five primaries in a row and people had begun to want him out of the race. Nancy didn't want him embarrassed. She would have been much happier if he had gotten out then. His political instincts, however, told him that this was not the end. When I went to North Carolina where they were campaigning, Nancy immediately grabbed me and began telling me I ought to tell Ron to get out of the race. Reagan came in and thought I was telling Nancy that he should drop out. He said, "Lyn, I'm not going to get out of the race. I'm going to stay in this thing to the end."

Yes, some of it is due to the fact that he is a fighter. He didn't want to leave on a losing note. But in addition, he knew and we knew that there were a lot of people in this country who wanted Ronald Reagan to be President. He was fighting overwhelming odds by running against a sitting Republican President, but he sensed that it wasn't over. He has made some tough political decisions as well as the tough decisions of the president.

Ronald Reagan has certainly been a unique figure in the politics of the United States since World War II. Whether he was a great president, I can't tell you. I don't think his second term was as good as his first term, but in many ways he is a man for all seasons. He is a man you can trust; he is a man you can believe; he is a man who doesn't take himself too seriously; he is a man who never got a fat head because he became an important person.

I have known four or five presidents, and I can tell you this: Ronald Reagan was not the smartest of them, but also not the least intelligent. He is a man whose qualities endear him to people. He is a man who has the one important quality of a president: he can make a decision. You have to be able to make decisions if you are a president, whether they are right or wrong. Jimmy Carter's problem was that he had a tough time making a decision. Ronald Reagan never had that problem. He can make a decision, and I think that's what made him a successful president. Thank you very much.

QUESTION: Mr. Nofziger, you said that President Carter was administratively more concerned about the trees than the forest, and that President Reagan was the opposite. Your illustrations about President Reagan as a caring person had most to do with his concern for individuals. However, with respect to groups or classes, or the unemployed he seemed particularly unconcerned. Should not the chief executive be more focused on the forest than on the trees in his caring, as well as in his administration?

MR. NOFZIGER: I think that a president, being a human being, ought to care about groups as well as individuals. But it is easy to say that Ronald Reagan didn't care about people as a mass because that's what you read in the papers. If you look at the record, social programs were not cut. They did not rise as fast as they had been rising, but they were not cut under Ronald Reagan. As far as I am concerned, he did care about people in the mass, but it is very hard to demonstrate that a man cares about people in mass unless he raises the budget to help people. There are those, however, who believe that the hand of Big Brother helping people is not necessarily the best way to go. He believed that the individual in the community also had a duty to help his fellow man, that it was not just the government's responsibility.

QUESTION: I wonder sir, if you have any insights on the chemistry between Reagan and Gorbachev?

MR. NOFZIGER: Yes. Here I go again with individuals. When he was first scheduled to meet with Gorbachev, there was a lot in the papers about Reagan giving the store away. That was a concern among a lot of conservatives, including myself. I called down to the White House and said that I wanted to see the President. They let me see him alone in the living quarters. I went in and said, "Mr. President, I'm speaking for a lot of concerned conservatives who are worried that you are going to give the store away." He said, "Lyn, stop. I don't want you to worry. I still have scars from when I was fighting the Communists in the movie industry, and I understand them. I'm not going to give anything away." Having said that there is no question that he and Gorbachev hit it off. But you know, Reagan hits it off with most people. If you give him a chance, he will be your friend. You have to be antagonistic toward him before he will become antagonistic toward you. He had a very good relationship with Gorbachev, who apparently is also a very charming man.

QUESTION: What are the qualities that President Reagan expected and valued most in his staff and those close to him? You indicated before that loyalty is one.

MR. NOFZIGER: He expects loyalty. He is not seeking loyalty; he thinks anybody who works for him is going to be loyal to him. In addition, he expects them to be competent; he expects them to be able to handle the details of government because he is not going to handle them. I can't even say that he expects them to share his political beliefs. Although he brought in people who he knew didn't share his beliefs, he expected that they would be loyal to him and carry out his wishes.

QUESTION: Do you think that Ronald Reagan would have opposed Jerry Ford in the 1980 race had Ford been elected in 1976?

MR. NOFZIGER: No, I don't think he would. Had Ford been elected President, I think Ronald Reagan would have been out there campaigning for him. Remember that after Ford became President, one of the first things he said was, "I will not seek election to another term." Beyond that, Reagan felt that Ford had never been elected vice president, or president, and therefore had not really earned the job. Ronald Reagan felt he had as much a right to seek the presidency as Gerald Ford did. There is no question in my mind, however, that had Ford been elected, we would have been out there working for him in the primaries.

QUESTION: Mr. Nofziger, when you were in the White House you must have had an opportunity to observe George Bush. Would you care to compare George Bush as a personality and an administrator with Ronald Reagan?

MR. NOFZIGER: I think George Bush is a much more hands-on administrator than Ronald Reagan was. He spent eight years observing Reagan's strengths and weaknesses and has tried to benefit from them. I think that George Bush has changed some as a politician over those eight years. He is a little more laid back, a little less excitable than he was. I think he learned from Reagan that you don't have to get all overwrought about things. George Bush, issues aside, has been a very effective president. He gives the appearance of being a stronger president than he did vice president. He is a little more low key; his voice doesn't hit those high notes; his wrists don't flap quite as much. I think he has handled his job of the presidency, in the perspectives of others, very well.

QUESTION: I cannot recall the members of any other administration accepting British honors at the end of their terms. Do you know anything about the acceptance of these honors by Ronald Reagan and Caspar Weinberger?

MR. NOFZIGER: I don't know anything about it. My own feeling is if I had been asked, I would have said, "I don't think it is quite proper." On the other hand, I don't think it is proper for a former president to go out and take money for speeches and those sorts of things. I frankly am a little disappointed there. I think the ex-presidency, like the presidency, is unique in the world. We have to be very careful to keep the standards of the office of ex-president, as it were, very high. If you look at Richard Nixon, whether you like him or not, he has never taken a nickel for making speeches since he has been out of office. I think that he has handled that office with a dignity and stature that Gerald Ford, Jimmy Carter, and Ronald Reagan have not.

NARRATOR: This certainly has been one of the most informative of all the Reagan oral history sessions. Thank you very much.

II

REAGAN AS LEADER:

VIEWS FROM OUTSIDERS

CHAPTER 5

THE REAGAN PRESIDENCY: MOMENTS

FRED BARNES

NARRATOR: Fred Barnes is the senior editor of the *New Republic*. He received his bachelor's degree in history from the University of Virginia in 1965. He went to the Charleston, South Carolina, *News & Courier* as a reporter, then returned and did graduate work at George Washington University. He went on to the *Washington Star*, where he was a writer for twelve years. He joined the *Baltimore Sun* in 1979 and continued until 1985. His work on the *New Republic* and "The McLaughlin Group" followed. He is the host of a radio show, a Voice of America program, "Issues in the News." Every Thursday he and Morton Kondracke tape a debate program called "Op Ed" for INN television. He is working on a book on the political culture of Washington and how it has changed since the time of JFK. In his spare time he does many other things such as write for *Reader's Digest* four times a year and more recently has written a column on politics for *Vogue* magazine.

Following the pattern of inviting journalists and scholars to discuss the Reagan presidency, it seems natural given Mr. Barnes writings over the last eight years that we turn to him to try to learn a little more from his vantage point about the Reagan presidency.

MR. BARNES: Thank you. I am delighted to be here. I had not visited U.Va. after I graduated in 1965 for 20–25 years, and now my daughter goes here. I've come back a lot of times since then, actually.

93

Ken has given me questions, some of which I am going to touch on, but I also have some other things that I would like to talk about. I'll touch on most of these questions. If not, I'll go back and answer a couple of them. What I thought I'd talk about are the differences between Reagan and Bush and the Reagan side of these differences, obviously. You can see Bush every day and you know what he is doing. Reagan you forget a little bit. It is amazing how quickly people forget even though it seemed as though Reagan was President forever.

Reagan was and is a passive person, but he had a very active presidency. Bush is a very active person, works on 20 or 25 things a day, but has a very passive presidency. Reagan had an amazing knack for never knowing more than he needed to. He usually knew just enough; sometimes he was a little short. I remember probably the worst briefing Reagan ever gave was one when he announced his decision on the MX missile in 1983. The first question, which was not even technical, he had to turn over to Cap Weinberger to answer because he just didn't know the details of the missile-basing system. But usually Reagan knew just enough to get by and not a whole lot more, which is actually very much like a journalist.

After 20 years I figured out how you can do just enough reporting of just the amount you need and no more. You can use your time a lot more wisely that way. It is also just like an actor, who learns just the lines he is going to use and doesn't learn any more. They don't do any extra work.

Reagan, of course, got his information from some unusual places for a president. Until the day he left the White House he always read *Human Events* every week. *Human Events* is a conservative weekly newspaper that is put out by some folks in Washington, and Reagan had read it for years and years. There were different phases in the Reagan presidency when aides tried to stop sending issues of the paper into him every week and Reagan would always ask for it, and always get it.

It affected policy in a number of ways. The last one to have a dramatic effect on Reagan was in the whole subject of the federal pay raise for members of Congress, members of the administration, and particularly federal judges. This was just as Reagan left in January 1989. He endorsed the 50 percent pay raise for members of Congress (the one that did not pass), and Bush also endorsed it. The reason Reagan endorsed it was because he had learned through

Human Events (whether this is right or wrong, I don't know, but I think it's probably wrong) that the conservative judges he had appointed to the federal judiciary would be leaving office in surprisingly large numbers unless the pay were raised. I don't think that would have happened, but in any case there was an article in *Human Events* saying that it would, and as a result Reagan was strongly in favor of the pay raise. Of course, Reagan himself had to send the recommendation. He could have sent a recommendation for 10 percent or a 20 percent pay raise, or no pay raise at all. It was really his call; he'd gotten the recommendation from a commission.

Reagan certainly did show that the job was not necessarily a 10, 12, or 16 hour a day job. Reagan arrived at nine and usually didn't stay around for lunch, and then came back in the afternoon for a while. He was not the hardest working guy I've ever run across in politics or government. Reagan was great when he was out campaigning for President in 1984 or 1980, or 1976 for that matter, because he'd do the main event for television and he might do something in the afternoon, maybe not. Sometimes he'd give a speech in the evening, sometimes not. You could usually skip it; he wouldn't say anything, it would just be a standard speech. So it was very leisurely coverage: leisurely campaigning, leisurely coverage, but enough for television and enough for a story in the newspapers every day. Reagan said a number of times in speeches that he had been told that hard work wasn't fatal but his attitude was, so why take a chance?

Rowland Evans, the columnist who is the partner of Bob Novak, tells a story about having lunch with Reagan. It must have been in 1987. Reagan would have lunch occasionally with journalists—I went to one of them—in the little study by the Oval Office. On the way out he was chatting with Reagan and looked up at him and said, "You know, Mr. President, I've known you for more than 20 years. I first met you in 1966 when you were running for governor of California, and the amazing thing is that you don't look any older now than you did back then. How do you do it?"

Reagan has a story for every occasion, and he said to Rollie Evans—and I've heard this from Rollie—"Let me explain it this way. Let me tell you the story of the two psychiatrists—the old psychiatrist and the young psychiatrist—who had a practice together. They'd come into their office every day just bubbling with enthusiasm, always happy, upbeat, smiling and chipper. Then they'd go into their separate suites and have patients come in and lie on the couch all day and talk about the woes in their lives. At 6:00 p.m. they'd come out and the young psychiatrist would be devastated, wiped out by the day, with a stomach ache, and just miserable. The old psychiatrist would be just as chipper and smiling and upbeat as he was when he went in that morning. This went on for a number of months. Finally one day they came out at 6:00 p.m., the young psychiatrist devastated as usual, and the old psychiatrist just as happy and smiling as he was when went in. The young psychiatrist stopped him and said, 'I don't understand it. We do the same thing every day, and I leave wiped out by hearing patients all day, and you come out after patients have been streaming in and out of your office just as upbeat as ever. How do you do it?' The old psychiatrist paused a minute and said, 'I never listen.'" Now remember, this is Reagan's explanation for how he keeps that youthful look.

In talking about the point of Reagan being a passive person and an active president, I had thought at least around the end of Reagan's first term, which was clearly superior to his second term in almost every way, that Reagan would be the big story of the late 20th century in the world, that he would be the most important historical figure. That obviously was before communism began to come completely unhinged during Reagan's second term, something that he had a little bit to do with but obviously not that much. That's obviously eclipsed Reagan, historically, as the important thing that happened in the late 20th century. But nonetheless Reagan did do a lot of things that will be regarded by future historians as very important.

These are things that Jimmy Carter certainly would have done, although I rather doubt if George Bush would have done them. The first is the deployment of the Pershing missiles in Europe in 1983. When the missiles were deployed, the Soviets immediately walked out of the arms control talks in Geneva and didn't come back for several years. The State Department, most everyone in Washington and the press, were hysterical, as they often are anyway.

One of the amazing things about Reagan, and one of the traits that is the least commented on, was his amazing ability to just block out the buzz in Washington and in the rest of the world for that matter. You could have a firestorm going on in Washington, and unless it went on month after month the way Iran-contra did, Reagan could just block it out and not pay any attention to it. The *Post* could be running these hysterical stories every morning about the fate of the world, of the arms control talks having broken down and the Soviets having walked out. The State Department types would be upset, Congress would be going crazy, the Democrats would be criticizing him, and the White House press would be clobbering his press secretary every day as Larry Speakes said at the briefings. Reagan would just be blissful and could just block it out completely, which is ordinarily, though not always, a great trait.

Of course he was vindicated entirely, I think, in blocking it all out over the Russians leaving the arms control talks. He always said, "Well, they'll come back," and of course they did.

The Pershing deployment was tied to the zero option that he proposed for eliminating medium-range nuclear missiles in Europe. Zero on both sides—the Soviets would eliminate the SS-20s and we would eliminate the Pershings. It was proposed initially that we wouldn't deploy the Pershings, but the proposal—the zero option—was not taken seriously. It was not taken seriously by most people in the administration, certainly by nobody in Washington. But Reagan stuck with it for six years, and finally it wound up being the INF Treaty.

The one thing Reagan disliked more than anything else were tepid, halfway proposals. Reagan liked a proposal where there was a pot of gold at the end of the rainbow. He liked sweeping proposals, for example, a proposal where no medium-range nuclear missiles were left—not a hundred on each side, but zero. Tied with that, Reagan liked proposals that had clear and palpable political appeal, and this one obviously did. We are eliminating nuclear weapons—that's a popular thing—and it is not surprising to me that when Richard Perle came up with this, Reagan grabbed it immediately. You can trace through the proposals of the Reagan administration, and most of the major ones were sweeping and very politically appealing, such as the 1981 tax cut that Reagan proposed (originally 30 percent cut, then 25 percent).

I would have loved to have been at the meeting in California in January of 1980 when Reagan was first briefed on supply-side economics. Jack Kemp, Jude Wanniski, and Art Laffer—about three-fifths of the whole supply-side movement—were there. Reagan for years had been talking about government. He attacked government size and government spending. That was basically the Reagan speech. It was an antigovernment speech, but it had limited political appeal because what Reagan was talking about was essentially taking something away from people: taking benefits away, shrinking the size of government. It had been basically what Republicans have been arguing about from the New Deal on: The government is doing too much, spending too much; we are going to withdraw it, that's what we want to do.

Reagan sensed the fact that this had limited political appeal, and his eyes must have widened immediately to the possibilities when supply-side economics was described to him. With tax cuts people get something. Reagan had never been that great a tax cutter before the 1980 campaign. His big issues in 1976 when running against Gerald Ford for the Republican nomination were opposition to the Panama Canal Treaty, anticommunism, and criticism of Henry Kissinger. In 1980 it was different; he was talking about reducing the size of government, but particularly cutting taxes. People were going to get something. You had with the tax cuts a sweeping proposal that would reduce tax rates ultimately by 25 percent; that was politically appealing.

I think at some point Jude Wanniski claimed that Reagan immediately and instinctively knew the appeal of reducing marginal tax rates. Jude has written about Reagan's talking so many times—at least in the 1980s—about the practice in Hollywood where an actor would do four or five movies and have three or four months left in the year. He would not do any more because the income tax rate on the later income would be too high, depending on what the rate back in the forties was.

At some point along the way, Reagan learned what he thought was another benefit of the tax cut: the strategic deficit. Reagan never used that phrase. To my knowledge David Stockman never used it, though Pat Moynihan, the senator from New York, claims he did. The strategic deficit, being a permanent deficit, has one particular effect, and that is to preclude the possibility of new spending programs. As Phil Gramm used to talk about it, you cut taxes to starve the spending. The strategic deficit still works. Reagan, while he would never concede that it was a goal that he achieved, was happy about it and knew perfectly well what was going on.

Then there was the Strategic Defense Initiative, which was almost a one-man band, entirely Reagan's doing, except that there is a great story that somebody is going to have. Maybe Edmund Morris or Lou Cannon will have in their books the story about how Reagan came to propose it in March 1983. Edward Teller and Bud McFarlane played a role. James Watkins, now the energy secretary in the Bush administration, was then, I believe, the chief of naval operations; he played a role. Richard Perle didn't play a role, even though he later became the greatest defender in the administration of "Star Wars." He was out of the country at the time. When the speech was prepared, Weinberger and Perle, who were in Spain, urged that the part about "Star Wars" be taken out entirely. Of course Reagan left it in.

Again, think of "Star Wars" and think of the way Reagan described it. Reagan really believed that this was going to make nuclear weapons obsolete. It had the double-barreled appeal: It was a sweeping proposal and had tremendous political appeal, because any poll shows that the American people think we ought to be defended against nuclear attack. Between 60 and 80 percent of the American people don't buy the idea of mutual assured destruction. That is something for the global thinkers to subscribe to, but the average American thinks that since the other guys have nuclear weapons, we ought to have a defense. SDI appeals to that viewpoint.

"Star Wars" also turned out to be—and sometimes these things are not entirely unintended consequences—the greatest bargaining chip ever in the history of arms control, and maybe in the history of the bargaining period. I think it probably more than anything else prodded the Soviets into almost every concession that they proposed, and there have been a lot of them now in arms control negotiations.

Look what happened just this week: Eduard Shevardnadze, the Soviet foreign minister, declared that the Krasnoyarsk radar site was a clear violation of the ABM Treaty. That was done, I believe, entirely to get the Soviets fully behind a strict interpretation of the ABM Treaty in a way that would ban serious testing and certainly deployment of "Star Wars" at a future date. Actually, Shevardnadze undercut a number of Democratic congressmen and Teddy Kennedy and people like that who had been denying for years that Krasnoyarsk was a violation of the ABM Treaty. Shevardnadze said it was a clear violation of the ABM Treaty, but the Soviets are still obsessed with getting rid of the Strategic Defense Initiative. The reason is pretty obvious: They can't keep up with it or match it. They don't have the computer capability. It is a fantastic bargaining chip now and was during Reagan's term.

Then you think of Grenada, which the Pentagon didn't want to invade, and Reagan did. The two bombings of Libya were the same, although the Pentagon wasn't quite as opposed to those. The capture of the *Achille Lauro* terrorists, who killed Leon Klinghoffer, is another example. All of those things are interventionist moves that Reagan liked.

Compare them with Bush and Panama. [Mr. Barnes spoke on 26 October 1989, prior to the invasion of Panama.] You have a cautious Secretary of State Baker saying, "Gee, there were such rapidly changing events," and so on. Reagan always wanted to go ahead. In those three cases it turned out pretty well. In Lebanon when he deployed troops, it didn't turn out so well.

One thing about Reagan that I think was widely believed was that Reagan would not know when, if a hard-line, anti-Soviet policy succeeded, to say, "Hey, let's talk. Now is the time to make concessions to embrace the Soviets and embrace Gorbachev." In fact, Reagan did know when the right time was. In other words, the theory behind a hard-line foreign policy toward the Soviet Union is that it is a way to get them to make concessions and ultimately to reach some agreement. We won't have a war. Reagan realized that.

The President embraced Gorbachev at exactly the point when he didn't have to. Reagan had been reelected in 1984 overwhelmingly; he wasn't going to run for another term; he was very, very popular; and he basically won the argument about whether he had to go back to the bargaining table with the Soviets. Most polls show that the American people think you ought to bargain, but Reagan hadn't done it for two years and had gotten away with it. At that point he embraced Gorbachev at the Geneva Summit in November 1985. He liked Gorbachev and went on from there with later summits in Washington, Reykjavik, Moscow, and so on. These were basically the highlights of his second term.

Reagan's second term was a downer for a number of reasons. One is that Reagan got old. Reagan would have good days and bad days. You saw him in June of 1988 when he went to the summit in

Moscow. I happened to go over and cover that; Reagan was in great shape. But there would be whole days and even weeks during the last couple of years where he would be kind of down in the dumps and a little out of it. At times it seemed his mind had already moved to California where he was going to go after he got out. He would sort of go in and out.

The one thing I know gave Reagan pleasure in his second term were Soviet stories that he would collect. I'm sure Edmund Morris would know where Reagan got all these Soviet jokes. Reagan claimed that all these stories—and I probably heard 10 or 15 of them from him at one time or another in speeches and other things—were tales that the Russian people would tell each other. They were very cynical about life in the Soviet Union.

My favorite one is the one that Reagan would tell about the Soviet citizen and the American citizen having a debate in Moscow over whose country had the most democracy. The American says, "Well, this is ridiculous. Why should we debate this? Everybody knows America has more democracy than the Soviet Union. We elect our leaders; if we don't like them, we vote them out of office. The Soviet Union is a totalitarian dictatorship. In Washington I can go over to the White House, walk into the Oval Office, go right up to the President's desk and say, 'President Reagan, you are doing a lousy job.'"

Well, to the surprise of the American, the Russian was not taken aback by this at all, and his response was, "Well, gee, we have that much democracy in the Soviet Union here in Moscow. I can go over to the Kremlin, march right up to the general secretary's office, go right up to his desk and say, 'President Reagan is doing a lousy job.'"

Reagan also used to tell the one about the guy who had been in a bread line in the Soviet Union. This guy had been standing in a line for more than an hour when he got furious and finally stormed off and said, "I've had enough. I can't stand this any more. I'm going to shoot Gorbachev." So he goes off and is gone for about an hour, and finally comes back. They said, "What happened? Did you shoot Gorbachev?" He said, "No, I went over to the Kremlin and the line is even longer over there."

Well, Reagan has about 10 or 15 of those, and I'd love to know exactly where he got them. He swore these were the real things, which I doubt, but that's what he said.

The first difference I'm suggesting is that Reagan was a passive person—certainly passive in his friendships. He would be extremely close to aides working for him, but the day they'd leave they'd never hear from him again. Reagan, I think, is a guy like a number of political figures in Washington who has no friends in the sense that most men or women have close friends. Nancy has a lot of friends. All their friends in Hollywood, the people they socialize with, are Nancy's friends. Ronald Reagan has political associates, political underlings, and world leaders whom he has appeared with, but doesn't have any friends. He doesn't have people who he can just call on and chat with. Bush has too many friends. But I can't think of anybody, including Reagan's brother, who is a close friend, and there is certainly nobody who Reagan really opens up to except for Nancy. Nancy is certainly a very close friend.

NARRATOR: You know Edmund Morris's explanation of that, don't you? It stems from his movie background because Reagan, and any principal actor, is very close to the people with whom he is working on a given movie, but when the movie is over, he goes on to another movie and repeats the same process there.

MR. BARNES: Yes, others have cited that as well, and I think there is probably something to that theory about Reagan. In any case, he is a very passive person but had a very active presidency.

The second difference is that Reagan was confrontational with Congress and with his political opponents, and he loved it. Bush is a compromiser. Reagan didn't like to have personal clashes with people. He loved to get along with Tip O'Neill when he would come in and chat, but he loved to fight Democrats in general in Congress—fight the liberals and fight the communists, and all these things. He really loved confrontation. Bush hates confrontation; he would rather compromise on anything. Bush's idea is to compromise first; Reagan's idea was to compromise at the last possible moment, and Reagan was a lot more effective as a result.

Think of what Reagan would be doing today in the situation of the capital gains cut that Bush is supposedly fighting for, a cut that he talked about during the election campaign. I don't think you can construe his election victory as a mandate for a capital gains cut, but at least it was put forward and the public voted for him. Furthermore, it has been overwhelmingly voted in favor of in the House of Representatives, and Democrats will acknowledge that there are more than 50 senators who are in favor of it. It needs to have a clean vote on it rather than one where you need 60 votes to procedurally attach it to some other bill. Bush whines about, "Why don't they let it vote? Why don't they let this thing go through? Or why don't they put it on the reconciliation bill?" Reagan would be on national television; he'd be steaming. He'd be describing this in colorful terms about how many dollars are being denied the American people because this capital gains cut hasn't gone through.

Think of the contras and how many times Reagan confronted Congress on the subject of the contras in Nicaragua. Bush avoided it from the beginning. You can just run down a list of things. Reagan was extremely confrontational and enjoyed it very much.

Another obvious difference is that Reagan was a very ideological person. Some people have tried to describe him as a closet pragmatist. I don't think Reagan was at all; I think he was easily the most ideological president since I've been covering Washington (back to Lyndon Johnson). From reading I think he was the most ideological president ever. He had an agenda; it was a short agenda, but there were things on it that he cared deeply about: reducing taxes, cutting the size of government, building up the military, and having an assertive anticommunist American foreign policy. He didn't reduce the size of government, but he did make some headway on the other three, and that's exactly what Reagan really cared about.

Reagan was not the most and still isn't the most widely read guy in the world, but he had been affected deeply by some of the things that he read. What especially comes to my mind is *Witness*, the book by Whittaker Chambers. Reagan had read it a number of times. Tony Dolan—I don't know whether you've had him in or not—a White House speech writer for eight years, tells the story about going in and talking to Reagan. They were working on a speech, the "Evil Empire" speech actually, which was originally written for Reagan to deliver in London in 1982 or 1983 when he spoke to Parliament in London. Reagan didn't deliver it then, so he delivered it later to an evangelical gathering in Orlando. In any case Tony Dolan is another fan of *Witness* by Whittaker Chambers. He went into the room as they were working on the speech, and they were talking about *Witness*. In the first part of the book Whittaker Chambers is talking about his daughter's ear lobe, and

Tony Dolan started to recite some of it. Reagan just picked it up in midsentence and recited part of the introduction to *Witness*. He remembered the book very well; that's why Whittaker Chambers got a posthumous medal of freedom. If you read *Witness*, you will see that there is a phrase in there, something about the Soviet Union being the focus of evil in the world. That phrase is used in the "Evil Empire" speech, and Reagan goes on to actually use the phrase "evil empire."

There were things back in the 1950s that Reagan used to read, for example some conservative economists, which affected him deeply. As the head of the Screen Actor's Guild, his whole flirtation with Communists in Hollywood affected him deeply, reading *Witness* affected him, and he became an extraordinarily fervent anticommunist. I think the thing that really allowed him to move toward détente with the Soviet Union was the fact that he liked Gorbachev. He liked him a lot, and they hit it off.

Nancy Reagan claims in her book that it was her idea entirely to have the fireside chat. They went to the boathouse or whatever in Geneva during the November 1985 summit. They were supposed to chat for half an hour and they wound up chatting for 90 minutes. What actually happened was Bill Henkel, the chief advance man in Geneva, pleaded with the Reagans and said, "We need to do a run-through." Henkel, a very talented guy who was the brains behind Mike Deaver, believed that it was always better to take Reagan through his paces, choreograph it a little bit, and let him know what the stage was going to be like wherever he was. Nancy didn't want to do it. Henkel was given a hearing with Nancy, and she was adamant about not doing it. Henkel called up to make a last minute plea to Nancy, who was lying in bed at the time (and never got up) as he pleaded with her over and over again. He said, "It is important to do this. The whole outcome of these talks can depend on this," and finally she said, "OK."

So they went down to the boathouse, and then Nancy said, "You know, maybe they could have a chat here," but it happened after she had refused for several days to even look at the place ahead of time. Otherwise that fireside chat would not have happened. I give her only half credit; Henkel deserves a lot of credit.

In any case we know Bush is a pragmatist; he's not an ideological president. Bill Schneider of the American Enterprise

Institute refers to him as an "in-basket president," which I think is about right. Whatever somebody else has put in the in-basket when he arrives in the morning, he deals with. Reagan filled his own in-basket.

Fourthly, Reagan was a great wholesale politician, and Bush is a classic retail politician. For Reagan, his performance in public was the most important thing. He preferred to be appealing to a national audience on television, but not always. I mean it was important for him to do well in every speech.

Jim Lake was Reagan's press secretary in the 1976 campaign and then for half of the 1980 campaign until he got fired in February of 1980. He tells the story of being with Reagan in 1976 when they were flying into Tennessee, where Reagan was going to give a speech. It was fairly late in the campaign for the Republican nomination, and they were about 20 to 25 minutes from landing, and Lake was going to put out a press release. He went into Reagan's compartment to raise some issue with him. Jim told me later that this was the only time Reagan ever got mad at him. Reagan got flustered and said, "No, I'm busy. Can't you see I'm working on my speech? I have to work on this. Just go away. We will be there in 20 minutes and I have to give this speech." Reagan was madly working away getting his speech just right.

The thing is, that was the same speech that Reagan had given a thousand times before, and yet the performance was what mattered. He went over his speech again and again to get a little nuance that would be appropriate for Tennessee. He worked on it every time because the performance mattered.

Now there is a new version of Mike Deaver in the White House. He was brought in for President Bush from Las Vegas and is a Republican media consultant who makes TV ads for campaigns. He is a believer in something that he calls "moments," and he wants to create some moments for George Bush. You know these sort of epiphanies on television where it will just capture some moment that will be seared in the mind of the American people in a very appealing way. Reagan didn't need a guide to tell him about moments because Reagan created them. I don't remember where I was—although I was at U.Va. at the time—when John Kennedy was shot, but I remember exactly where I was during certain of Reagan's moments.

The first one was on 4 June 1984 when Reagan gave his speech at Normandy, the D-Day speech. I was staying in Los Angeles, and the California primary was coming up. I watched his speech early in the morning on television because Reagan was obviously nine hours away, and the speech was to survivors of American soldiers who had actually landed in Normandy. He talked about this one guy whose daughter was there. It was the most extraordinary speech I've ever heard. It had no news content whatsoever, he didn't advance any policy or anything, yet it was just extraordinary. Later, it became the bulk of the 18-minute film about Reagan that was shown at the Republican National Convention, easily the most powerful piece of political propaganda I have ever seen. There was a big flap over whether the networks should show it or not. Of course they should have shown it; they didn't, but they should have. It was just a fantastic piece of political propaganda. It was unbelievable. That's one moment.

The second one is Reagan and the families of the *Challenger* victims. The families assembled in Houston, and Reagan and Mrs. Reagan went down there. Reagan could do events like that as nobody else could. People denigrated it by saying he was a great ceremonial president. It was a lot more than just being a ceremonial president; it was capturing the right emotion, his ability to deal with people.

I remember sitting on my couch at home and watching a replay of the whole thing on C-Span, and I had to turn it off because it was so emotional. Reagan gave a speech that was written by Peggy Noonan, who was very good at writing these emotional speeches, but it was powerful the way Reagan acted.

The inconsequential public events are the ones they do with athletic champions: the World Series winner, the Super Bowl champs, or the NBA champs. I always go to those; they are fun to go to, particularly if you are a sports fan, and I am. You can go and mingle with these guys. But Reagan was tremendous with these teams at utterly inconsequential, ceremonial events. I remember the one when the 76ers came and presented Reagan with a jersey that had No. 1 on the front and Reagan on the back, and a basketball. While everybody was still standing there—this took place in the Rose Garden—and Reagan had the 76ers behind him, and all the press, the assembled friends and wives of the 76ers to the side. Reagan alone walked across the grass toward the Oval Office with the basketball. He threw it up in his hands, and then he looked over out the side of his head at the cameras and dribbled it once on the grass. If you've ever dribbled a basketball on the grass, you know that the ground is lumpy. The ball is just as likely to bounce away somewhere, but with Reagan it bounced right back. I always thought if it were Jimmy Carter, he would have dribbled it off his foot, because he was terrible at those events. But in this case, the ball bounced right up and Reagan kind of tossed it up and went on in. Reagan could do those kinds of things with the TV cameras on and the public watching him. That one in particular was a magnificent event of no consequence, but a moment that I remember very well because I had gone to it.

The fifth thing is that Reagan was and is a larger-than-life figure, and Bush is a smaller-than-life figure. Marlin Fitzwater, who eventually became Reagan's press secretary, claims that it didn't make any difference what Reagan said at all those press conferences. Do you remember the ones where he would bomb—at least all the reporters thought he would bomb—and they'd put out score cards saying Reagan had made 19 errors? Marlin believes to this day that it didn't make any difference, that there was such magic with Reagan's presence, his charisma, and his star quality that he could say anything and the American people would like him. I think that carries the whole idea of charisma to an extreme, but Marlin believes this entirely; he really does.

The other thing about Reagan that makes him a larger-than-life figure is mystery. There haven't been many figures with an air of mystery in my reporting career, but among the few were Ronald Reagan, Martin Luther King, George Wallace, and Richard Nixon (while not a charismatic person, Nixon was certainly a larger-than-life figure and one of the most peculiar people I've ever met). There has to be some mystery and some tension. There is not a whole lot of mystery with George Bush, and not a whole lot of mystery with most political figures in this country. There is no reason why there should be. But with Reagan there was a mystery and part of the mystery was what made one ask, "How does this guy do it?" There was tension there: How much does this guy know? Does he really know what he is doing? Is he just acting out some script that somebody has written for him? I don't think he was, but there was always tension there. Has he really got control of his job? Is he really in charge here? I've concluded that Reagan basically was, but still there was always tension, and it is still around as far as Reagan is concerned.

I had three or four private sessions with Reagan; the first one was in September of 1984. They brought about four or five journalists in. Patrick Buchanan was one, along with David Broder, myself, and a couple of others. Reagan was amazingly uncommunicative. He didn't say anything. I remember Broder asked him about Mondale. You know, just an ambiguous question like: "What do you make of this guy Mondale?" Reagan didn't say anything. This was supposedly completely off the record, but Reagan knew that nothing was ever really off the record if you are telling it to a journalist in Washington. And Reagan said practically nothing. I learned zilch from going.

Then when Patrick Buchanan got to the White House he arranged lunches for journalists there, and I got to go to the second one. Novak went to the first one. The second one included Morton Kondracke, who was then at *Newsweek* and now is back at the *New Republic*, and Paul Harvey, the radio personality. We were in a private off-the-record lunch, and Harvey was presenting himself as the spokesman for America to see the President. I thought we were there to have a luncheon chat, but Paul Harvey thought otherwise. In any case I sat right next to Reagan. For an hour and a half the only question that he even got animated about in answering was one I asked him about movies, whether he had seen any good movies lately. Reagan had some amazing stories about movies. He started off by telling me a story about a movie in Hollywood, a story he has told many times. It was exactly the same story I had heard back in August or September of 1984 when I had asked him about movies in that session with the other reporters.

One interesting thing happened when I saw him in September 1984. We were leaving and I asked him if he had seen the movie "Red Dawn." Most of you probably are familiar with this movie, but I don't go to many movies. I try to go to movies that from my standpoint, being pretty conservative, are politically correct. That means I don't go to many movies. But in any case "Red Dawn" is about a communist invasion of the United States. They seize a great chunk of the United States in the middle of the country, and then some teenagers stage a rebellion that eventually thwarts them. It's not a very good movie but kind of fun, and all the liberal critics naturally panned it. I asked Reagan if he had seen it, and he said,

"Yeah, I saw that movie. They got the plot entirely wrong. They should have redone the plot. It was crazy to have these guys rebelling. They couldn't have done that. They should have called for another army to come in, because we had an army on the West Coast, and that army should have come in, and then the teenagers would get together with the army and drive them out." He went on; he had a whole other plot for the movie. Actually, it would have made a better movie. That was the one interesting thing he said at that session. It's the only thing I remember, except that he didn't say anything about Mondale.

How frustrating Reagan can be for reporters! The most frustrated person I ever talked to about this was Bob Novak. Between 1976 and 1980 Reagan naturally went around and made a lot of speeches because he was thinking of running in 1980. Novak was going to do a column on him in 1978. He picked him up in Florida, and Reagan had a small private plane that was going to fly all the way to Oklahoma that night. It was going to take a long time in a small plane and Novak thought, "Boy, I'm going to have about three hours sitting next to this guy. I'm going to pump him for everything I've wanted to know for years. This isn't going to be just one column; I'm going to get ten columns out of this." He got no columns out of it, as it turned out. He said that the only thing Reagan would talk about on which he would say anything was movies. He talked on and on about movies, all the old Errol Flynn stories, and stories about Robert Taylor. Reagan loved to talk about that stuff, but Novak got nothing out of him and was incredibly frustrated as a result.

I covered the Reagan administration, but I didn't serve in it. Are there other questions?

QUESTION: What was Reagan like in private company? Did you have a chance to evaluate him?

MR. BARNES: Yes, I think Reagan was charming but not interesting. He was much more interesting in public than he was in private. He didn't have much to say and didn't want to say much. He didn't want to talk about himself a lot and reveal much. He certainly never did to journalists, and I don't think he did to others either. It would be a lot of small talk and not much more than that.

From talking to other people who dealt with him, that's the best I can answer.

NARRATOR: Is that any different than other politicians who try to conceal themselves, who have strategic reasons for not revealing themselves?

MR. BARNES: Most politicians are pretty talkative about themselves and reveal more than you want to know sometimes. You don't feel, with most of them, that there is a wall there. If you are in journalism, usually they want to put their best face forward; they want you to like them. They want you to write favorably about them; they are charming and interesting in private, usually. When you've seen a politician in public, you've heard him give the same speech a number of times, and when you get with him in private it is a lot more interesting. There is fresh material there. With Reagan there was no fresh material. You've already had his best stuff, and it is not as interesting in private. He's not a guy I'd want to spend a lot of time with except for the fact that he is a charming person. I wouldn't want to spend a lot of time discussing geostrategic affairs or the election of 1992 and who is going to run or win, and so on. With Nixon, you could sit around and talk about those kinds of things for hours. Reagan wouldn't have much to say; it would be pretty pedestrian.

QUESTION: You refer to his second term as something of a downhill.

MR. BARNES: Well, it was.

QUESTION: Old age set in. How about the impact of the Iran-contra?

MR. BARNES: That's another thing, obviously. You had several things that came along: he got old, the Democrats took over the Senate, and right on the heels of that, a day or two later, Iran-contra broke. That created a buzz in Washington and around the country that went on for so many months that Reagan couldn't ignore it. He couldn't just block it out, and that took a lot out of him. He dropped 20 points in the polls, and there is the famous story of what he said to Bob Dole. Bob Dole said something about fans, and Reagan said, "Well, you may have fans; I don't have any fans anymore." He was really downtrodden, down in the dumps. That was the only time in his entire presidency when Reagan was down in the dumps. It was in the spring—late winter and spring. Don Regan was getting fired, and Nancy was manipulating everybody or trying to. She denies a lot of it in her book, but I expected that. Reagan had surgery in January of 1987.

QUESTION: Was he a man to stick with old friends? I'm thinking of Meese.

MR. BARNES: Meese was not a friend; Meese was an employee. Meese had worked for him as governor of California, but there was not a peer relationship with him. Nancy didn't like Ed Meese; she says so in her book. I think every other Cabinet member and his wife or her husband was invited to a private dinner at the residential part of the White House. Ed Meese was never invited there to a private dinner with the Reagans.

QUESTION: Did he have any affection for any of his political colleagues?

MR. BARNES: He had a lot of affection for them, but it was "out of sight, out of mind." He had great loyalty, but it was political loyalty, not personal loyalty. He stuck with Meese. Remember that during the entire period when Meese had been nominated for attorney general and there was a special prosecutor investigating him (it went on for a year), Reagan was under great pressure to jettison the nomination. He never flinched. It never occurred to him really to drop it; he was going to stick with Meese because that's what you did. But that was political loyalty; it wasn't particularly personal loyalty, I don't think.

QUESTION: If they weren't personal friends, why was he so reluctant to fire people who should have been fired?

MR. BARNES: He was reluctant to fire anybody. Why was Jimmy Carter reluctant to fire people? Why doesn't George Bush fire people? It is hard to do, and presidents don't like to do it.

Something odd happens in the White House. These guys can't fire anybody. I don't know why. While Reagan reveled in public political confrontations, he didn't like personal confrontations with anybody, and Bush doesn't either for that matter.

COMMENT: As I remember it, during the first year of the administration, there were repeated stories about a gang of half a dozen Los Angeles millionaires who were supposed to be his top advisers.

MR. BARNES: It was the kitchen cabinet.

QUESTION: Were they not friends?

MR. BARNES: Not really. These were Justin Dart, and Earle Jorgenson, and Holmes Tuttle. They were friends, but not close friends. Basically these were the people who, after Reagan's speech in 1964 for Goldwater, decided, "Aha, this is a hot political property. Why don't we run him for governor?" That's when they got to know Reagan. That's when they raised money and ran Reagan for governor. They became friends, but it was basically a political association. They weren't friends in the way that we normally think of friends, that is, someone you may have known from college whom you've stayed in touch with all these years, confiding in them and asking their advice about personal things. I don't think they were friends like that. Furthermore, the White House staff really shut them out in terms of having any influence. You can imagine how much Jim Baker, Ed Meese, or Mike Deaver wanted these rich guys out in California shaping the policy of the Reagan administration. They made sure they weren't doing that. They saw Reagan very little, and so far as I know, Reagan never said, "Where are all my buddies from LA? Why haven't I been talking to them?" If he said it, I never heard of it.

COMMENT: They are the same gang who got together to buy him the house that he is in now.

MR. BARNES: Some of them are the same ones.

QUESTION: I wonder if you'd like to comment on this situation. At the Versailles economic conference the G-7 leaders agreed to certain things that had been laid out previously. They'd hardly gotten back home when President Reagan clamped down on the French and others for wanting to go ahead and build the gas pipeline for Russia. There was a great deal of unemployment at the time and General Electric was involved, and yet Reagan threatened to take them to court. Why would a man make such a diversion from cooperation to threatening to sue everybody?

MR. BARNES: I really don't know, and here is my excuse for not knowing. The things I usually know about are the things I actually reported on. I never wrote anything on the whole pipeline controversy. I didn't go to that particular economic summit. Frankly, I just don't remember it that well, so I don't have any personal knowledge of why Reagan did that. It might be that he just didn't understand what it meant. The pipeline thing was a vestige of Reagan's long-standing anticommunism, and he just didn't think it was a good idea. Reagan would be forced to say things in public that he didn't really believe. For instance, Reagan said some things publicly about Iran-contra, and he didn't believe them at all. That can make diplomacy awfully difficult.

QUESTION: I have always wondered since the first Iran-contra publicity why Reagan didn't get his team together right away, find out what happened, go on TV and tell the people, take the responsibility, and say we were trying to get the hostages out. We learned something that we probably should have known already—that bargaining in the Middle East is a very complicated affair. But instead he kept quiet.

MR. BARNES: He didn't keep entirely quiet. Here was the problem: Oliver North, Bud McFarlane, and John Poindexter were all lying to Reagan and Bill Casey. They were concocting a story about what went on. This is a part of his problem of "over-delegation," which is something I didn't really touch on. During the first press conference he had (I believe on 19 November 1986), the amount of untruths and misinformation that Reagan stated was what he had gotten from Poindexter and Casey. I think that's the problem. Reagan was aloof from what was going on, and he was victimized by these people on his staff. I don't mean to absolve him; it was his own fault. But I think that's the explanation. He didn't know what the truth was, and they told him something that wasn't true.

QUESTION: With respect to initiatives, did he rely heavily on staff and advisers to suggest to him what he should do, or did he direct them to get the information to support what he wanted to do?

MR. BARNES: Well, all the things that I talked about were ones that Reagan initiated. You think Jim Baker would have gone for a deep, controversial three-year tax cut in 1981? He would have compromised for a third of that. SDI? Baker never did like it. The zero option, deploying the Pershings and all those things? Those are all the things that Reagan wanted to do. Grenada?

COMMENT: They were all his initiatives.

MR. BARNES: Yes. Grenada? Reagan wanted to do that. The Pentagon didn't want to do it; he had to order them to do it because the Pentagon doesn't want to fight anywhere these days.

That's why I think when books come out like the one by Bob Schieffer and Gary Paul Gates, *The Acting President*, that characterize Reagan as a guy just completely aloof from what was going on, you can cite examples of that—Iran-contra is one with the problems Reagan got into. But on other things, on the most important things that went on in his administration, Reagan was the driving ideological force. He instigated them. They didn't just come out of thin air. SDI didn't, and it was all Reagan's doing to put that in the speech and embark on that initiative.

QUESTION: What did you think about his relationship with his daughter Patty, who wrote the book about her dad? Did this bother him very much? He was always talking about the importance of the American family life. His own family was such a contrast.

MR. BARNES: Reagan has a very weird family, I've always thought. I think the book bothered Nancy a lot more than it did Reagan, although he said he read it. I'm not sure whether he did or not. I haven't read her book.

One thing that comes through clearly in all of them is that Reagan is basically a terrible parent. He is not a good father. He is a charismatic leader, but he just didn't spend much time with his kids. His adopted son, Michael, was a football star at a prep school in Arizona. Reagan never went to see him play. He handed the job of disciplining the children entirely to Nancy, who is kind of a brittle person. He should have done a lot of it himself. Fathers and mothers need to do that, I think. That's the way it works in my house anyway, and it worked while I was growing up too. There is something missing in Reagan's personality. Maybe it was from his own experience with his father.

NARRATOR: Who was a drunk.

MR. BARNES: Who was a drunk. So Reagan didn't know what he needed to do. He never came home; he was basically an absentee father.

COMMENT: He talks so much about the importance of family life.

MR. BARNES: There is a certain hypocrisy there. They don't have a warm, chummy family life the way the Bushes do, for instance. Reagan will be remembered as a greater president, I am certain, but Bush will be remembered as a greater father.

NARRATOR: What do you think of the story that Reagan was traveling with Michael one time on a plane coming into Washington, and Reagan kept counting on his fingers. Michael said, "What are you doing?" and Reagan said, "I'm counting." He heard him say one, two, three, four, five, six, seven, eight, nine, ten. He said, "I'm counting. In ten months I'll be able to go to church again." Does that suggest something that runs counter to the proposition that Bush practices his values and Reagan really didn't have much seriousness about values in that area?

MR. BARNES: You mean in religion?

NARRATOR: Conventional religion.

MR. BARNES: I've always been mystified about Reagan's religion. I was on the panel of the first Reagan-Mondale debate in 1984 and I asked a question. If you remember the format for these debates, you asked a question and a follow-up of one candidate, and then roughly the same question and a follow-up to the other candidate. In October of 1984 the whole question of religion and politics was being discussed; Reagan had appeared at various religious events, and Mondale had talked a lot about his father, who was a minister. Religion had been in it, so I thought this was a perfectly legitimate question: "Do you consider yourself a born-again Christian, and in what way has your Christian faith affected your decision making in the White House?" He gave me some empty answer, and I asked the follow-up question: "Why don't you go to church? You are a Christian; why don't you go to church?" I thought I had an airtight question. "Why don't you go to church or why don't you have a minister come in to the White House the way Richard Nixon did, or if you are at Camp David have one come there the way Jimmy Carter did?" Well, he gave this answer about how he didn't want to go to church because the church might get blown up or something. If he'd given that answer, it really would have precluded his doing anything in public, of ever giving a speech anywhere because there might be some terrorist attack. Reagan dodged the first question, and he didn't have a real response to the second one.

I've never understood Reagan's Christian faith. Reagan thinks that he is a deeply faithful Christian, yet most Christians I know, including myself, in the natural course of events go to church most of the time. You want to, and it's very natural; but Reagan doesn't seem to want to. Yet there are certain areas of Christianity that he has an almost obsessive desire to talk about, particularly the apocalypse, which is probably the area that I'm least interested in talking about. Some Christian leaders have talked to him. But to be honest I really don't know the state of Reagan's faith. I know what he thinks it is, but I'm not sure what it really is.

NARRATOR: What about Reagan's restraint during the KAL incident and other events? There have been cases, haven't there, where a true activist would have struck where he showed great restraint?

MR. BARNES: Well, it was a Korean plane, after all. It wasn't an American plane, so I'm not sure that it was that great a restraint.

The whole thrust of Hirsch's book—I don't know if it is correct or not—is that the White House and the Reagan administration exploited that affair and accused the Soviets of purposely shooting down a defenseless plane even after the White House knew that its shooting was basically accidental. In other words, they really did mistake it for an intruding spy plane.

NARRATOR: Leaving aside content, what about his capacity to write when he was rewriting a speech? Edgar Shannon, former president of the University of Virginia, tells a story that when they had reached an impasse in the Rockefeller Commission and they couldn't get a statement the way they wanted it, Reagan said, "Well, let me see what I can do." He excused himself, went out of the room, came back, and presented a recasting of the arrangement, and they said, "Well, this is exactly what we want."

MR. BARNES: He was a great editor. I've talked at great length to all the speech writers. I got to know some of them pretty well in Reagan's time. No president writes his own speeches, and they don't even work up a first draft. They are presented with a speech after some general ideas are tossed out. But Reagan could do some truly magical editing, putting in personal vignettes, adding jokes and all of the personal touches. All the Reagan things Reagan would put in himself, i.e., all the things that made his speeches good and memorable. For example, when Reagan gave State of the Union speeches, he'd have some hero sitting up in the balcony at the House of Representatives; one year he had that Vietnamese boat woman who was a cadet at West Point. That's the one I remember the best. The guy who dove in the Potomac and picked out some people and saved the guy from the Air Florida crash was a detail Reagan added to his speech. He could turn a drab piece of copy into a dazzling speech that would really hold your interest, not because of the content of the policy, but because of the Reagan touches, the vignettes, the stories, and the jokes.

COMMENT: Bush tried it but it backfired.

MR. BARNES: Bush can't do it; he is terrible on television, and he is not a performer at all. He can't effectively address the nation. But Bush is the norm, and Reagan is the exception. Jimmy Carter wasn't so great; Richard Nixon wasn't either; Gerald Ford wasn't; nor was Lyndon Johnson. There are not many politicians who have this ability to communicate on television the way Reagan did, and I guess Kennedy could.

The interesting thing is that Reagan sells books. Nobody would buy a book about Gerald Ford or Jimmy Carter. There is a certain audience for Richard Nixon, an anti-Nixon audience. But there is interest in Reagan given this dazzling figure, and books about him have sold, and of course books about Jack Kennedy and about the Kennedys still sell like crazy. But you can't give away books about Carter and Ford.

NARRATOR: One last question. Do you fellows feel as intensely as you speak on McLaughlin?

MR. BARNES: Oh, it depends on the issue sometimes. The one issue that got people, since I've been doing that show, was Iran-contra in general, but Oliver North in particular. The period when Oliver North testified before the Iran-contra Committee was even more emotional in particular. That was when there were probably the most disagreements on the "McLaughlin Group" since I've been on. Actually, I've known all those people on there for many years. Although I don't know John McLaughlin that well, Mort Kondracke and I have been friends for at least 15 years, and now we work together at the *New Republic*. Jack Germond was my boss at the *Washington Star* and was the guy who first assigned me to cover the White House and write about politics. This was back in the mid-1970s.

NARRATOR: Was his book on the election good?

MR. BARNES: I have read it. I've read all of his and Jules Witcover's books on the election. It has some good stuff in it, but I really think it needed to be more analytical. I found I wasn't that interested in the Iowa caucuses anymore. I'm waiting for a good book on the election. I read the *Newsweek* book and Germond and Witcover's book, and there's one by a couple of people on the

Boston Globe which dissects the Dukakis campaign and why it went limp. I haven't read it, but it is supposed to be pretty good. Then there will be some books by some of the actors involved. So far I'm waiting for a good book on the campaign. It was an interesting campaign so there ought to be a good book on it. In 1984, the campaign was so dull that there was no way you were going to have a good book. There was another good campaign in 1980, and Germond and Witcover had a very good book.

NARRATOR: We are terribly grateful that we could have this session. Now that you've found where we are, we hope you will come again.

CHAPTER 6

REAGAN AT THE CROSSROADS AGAIN: 1986

LOU CANNON

NARRATOR: Charles McDowell said recently that perhaps columnists had reached the point of diminishing returns, because more and more they seem to be answering one another rather than addressing the subject. Lou Cannon is a notable exception to that trend. In a review of *Ronnie and Jessie*, Lou Cannon's book on Ronald Reagan and Jessie Unruh, one reviewer had referred to the deeper contest that underlies all political competition. Cannon responded, "It is to this contest that my interest is addressed. I care a good deal, or think I do, about our political system, and my intention is to write books that contribute to the understanding of that system and those who inhabit it." That is seemingly the purpose of his columns. That's an objective that has inspired his writings from the days when he covered Ronald Reagan and the state capitol in California for the *San Jose Mercury-News,* through his latter writings on Reagan as president.

There is a thrust to Lou Cannon's writings that political scientists might imitate in trying to understand the nature and the functioning of the political system. More than he knows, those of us who follow the presidency and politics in general draw upon his writings as a source for understanding the political system.

Perhaps this can be explained by the fact that his career was broader than that of most writers. He was a truck driver for two years after college; he wrote for three smaller papers in the first three years of his career; he was a copy editor before becoming bureau chief in Sacramento for the San Jose paper.

MR. CANNON: Thank you for your very generous introduction. We were with Ronald Reagan last week in Grenada. The reporters in the pool asked him about the medical school. We went from point to point on the island where the U.S. troops had been in that little war. Of course, one of the high interest points of the trip was the St. George's Medical School where there were 800 American students who were rescued by our troops in this invasion. There, I've said it both ways—I've given the Reagan people "rescue" and I've given the rest of us "invasion." In any case, Reagan's party got to the medical school. The press secretary, Larry Speakes, was not with the President. He was attending a funeral in Mississippi. So Reagan was sort of on his own and they were letting him, as a result, answer many more questions than he usually is able to answer at these picture-taking sessions known as photo opportunities. So the reporters in the pool asked, "What do you think about being here at the medical school, Mr. President?" thinking they would get some historic reply about how wonderful it was to be at the site where 800 American students were rescued, as he had said in his speech. Reagan looks at the school a little wistfully and said, "That's a nice looking place. It sort of reminds me of California." That was it. It wasn't in my story. It probably won't be in your news magazine because none of us knew what to make of it.

I'm going to talk about Reagan at the crossroads in two ways. I'm going to talk about him as a president in the sixth year of his presidency, and I want to talk about the way he communicates. One is tempted to say that Reagan is always at the crossroads because he is on the one hand the most gifted television political communicator of our age and on the other, he is also a regular supplier of gaffes or what appear to be gaffes and sort of absentminded witticisms that keep me with a store of what I call "Reaganisms of the week." I don't believe the two things are as unrelated as people think.

First, I want to suggest where he stands in his policy. Recently, I wrote an article for the Outlook section of the *Post*. I began with a dire list of all of the things that faced Ronald Reagan: the problems he was going to have with the budget, the problems he was going to have with taxes, the problems he was going to have with foreign policy. The thrust of the piece was that finally the conflicting nature of Reagan's promises, particularly the promises to both raise the military spending to a level that he finds acceptable and cut taxes while balancing the budget, were going to come home to roost. It looked like a very compelling account of the problems facing the President; indeed it was, except it was written a year ago at the beginning of 1985. I gave speeches on Reagan at the crossroads then too. This year I maintain he really is there.

He also has some real opportunities this year. I think that there is also the possibility that his presidency is going to be seen as a popular time of good feeling, much as Eisenhower's presidency was, but not as a period of real accomplishment. His presidency will be marked in the history books as an interlude rather than as the new direction which he fondly believes it will be. I think we are going to know the answer to several of these questions at the end of the year.

In foreign policy, I think that the current situation in the Philippines is very important, even though Reagan put his foot in his own policy a week ago by his sort of offhand reference, first in an interview with the *Post* and then in a press conference, about there being fraud on both sides. I think that the Philippines actually does mark a new era in American policy in Asia, a new era of realism. This time the CIA did not take information from the government or "official sources" about how well everything was going. This time the military argued early: "Find another horse." This time a conservative senator was sent out to tell Marcos that he had to change his ways. While he did not know what the ending was going to be, we knew at least that the beginning was different. There was an attitude of realism toward despots, of which you also see in the providing of the plane for Mr. Duvalier, that I think is a welcome feature of our foreign policy.

In other words, I think that, despite the rhetoric of the President's 25 October speech to the United Nations, there is evidence of a kind of realism, a pragmatism even—to use that word so distrusted by some of Reagan's conservative supporters—evident in the White House. I think you are also going to see that in domestic policy.

The reason that Reagan is hard to understand, I believe, and the reason that he can continually confound his critics, dismay his supporters and stay interesting to us, lies in contradictory impulses of his character. He has this optimism, this spirit of Americanism, a forward-lookingness that makes him a young old man. But other people have this and are not quite as contradictory as Reagan. One of the paradoxes of Reagan is that he proclaims there are simple answers, but not easy ones. He is derided as simplistic, but is, in fact, very contradictory and complex. The contradictory impulses in Reagan are between his ideology and his tendency to compromise. Reagan is never completely satisfied nor completely understandable, because he is at once an ideologue and a pragmatist.

You see this in all sorts of ways. I've written two books on Ronald Reagan. [Four years after his discussion, Cannon published a third book.] When I wrote the second book I thought that I had a sort of running start. The first book had been easy. I thought the second would be easier; it was much harder. I thought that I didn't have to deal with the boyhood or the early years of Reagan because I had already done this. Most biographers have trouble with the log cabin phase of their hero's life. When you get right down to it, everybody had a mother and a father, and everybody from the most famous president of the United States to the local ax murderer had somebody who said, "I never knew that Johnny was destined for greatness." The other thing you find out is if you have the opportunity to interview people in Dixon, Illinois, as I did in 1968 and then again in 1980, the number of people who got to know Ronald Reagan when he was growing up between 1968 and 1980 is absolutely remarkable. Anyway, I found I didn't know Ronald Reagan at all, and that to understand him as President, I had to try to understand his character, because Ronald Reagan decided things from the heart.

For example, taxes are the issue about which Ronald Reagan is most ideological and least compromising. Why is that? It isn't because he was waylaid by Jack Kemp and brainwashed in a seminar with supply-siders somewhere. It's because Ronald Reagan grew up poor and made a lot of money in the late 1940s on the strength of a contract that had been signed for him on a film before he went into the service. The film was *King's Row*. When he came out, he was making lots of money when the marginal tax rate in the United States was 90 percent and individuals couldn't use the income averaging tax provision. Ronald Reagan went around—he was a liberal Democrat, mind you, not a conservative—saying to people, "We've got to have a human depreciation allowance like they have for the oil companies." He said once to a friend, "It wasn't an idea that caught on," but it is something that has always stayed with him. Taxes for him are an evil; he loathes them.

If you want to understand the Reagan presidency you have to understand Reagan. I found out in doing the second book about him that the key to Reagan is what is going on in his gut. That, I think, is why people like him.

Another experience that influenced Ronald Reagan was his years as a negotiator for the Screen Actors Guild. He led them in what was then their only successful strike. He was a very good negotiator. He believes that he lost some roles that he would have had because producers got sore at him. Maybe he's right; there is no way to prove that.

Ronald Reagan told me something once that I have never forgotten in writing about him; he said, "The purpose of a negotiation is to get an agreement." That has been in my head every time I write an arms control story, or every time I was told by various of his stalwart supporters in the first term that he would never meet with the Soviet leader, much less make a serious arms control proposal. What Reagan does is negotiate and compromise at the margins. This is the year when I think we can truly say that Reagan is at the crossroads, because this is the year that the ideologue and the negotiator are going to be most at war with one another.

I think I have to give Reagan a little on the economy. He says we don't call it Reaganomics anymore during the recovery; it's true—we don't. We called it Reaganomics mostly during another recession. People say that Reagan's popularity, like Eisenhower's, wasn't connected to his policies. They haven't looked at the polls. The low points for both Reagan and Eisenhower in their presidencies coincide with the lowest points of the economy in those presidencies and the period of the greatest unemployment. While Ronald Reagan will always be more popular than his policies, it isn't an automatic given. "Our polls," as Barry Sussman, the *Washington Post* pollster, likes to say, "don't show the Teflon." There is an intimate connection between the economy and the way Ronald Reagan is perceived.

If you accept the analysis, which I do, that unless there is some effort at deficit reduction made this year (not a balanced budget—we don't need a balanced budget—but we do need some sign that the deficit is going in the other direction) this is going to show up in the markets and Reagan's recovery will be jeopardized. This means that he would have to accept a whole mélange of issues, particularly the tax increase that is there waiting to be enacted. If Ronald Reagan were to whisper tax increase to one senator of either party, a tax increase would be handed to him within a week. He also needs some kind of restraints in the defense budget, which he is hoping to get help on from the Packard Commission, and some kind of domestic spending cuts. Ronald Reagan could make his call for domestic spending cuts stick if he is willing to show some restraint on the defense budget.

I think all of these things are going to come together late this year because the Supreme Court today agreed to review Gramm-Rudman. They are not expected to decide until July. You don't know very much about what this Congress will do, but one thing you know is it won't make a decision before it has to. This probably means that a decision will be made in the fall in an election year that will determine whether or not the Republicans control the Senate.

I think that Ronald Reagan will run out of running room. A lot of people have been predicting it since he first announced for office in California in 1966. Some day they will be right. At some point it's going to be true that Ronald Reagan has run out of negotiating room and is a lame duck. But I'm not going to bet the mortgage that that's going to be this year.

Let me just briefly talk about Reagan as communicator. First of all, I agree with my friend Mark Shields, who says that the term *Great Communicator* is used by Reagan's critics as a put-down and as a way for them not to understand Reagan. Reagan succeeds, Mark believes, because he has values, because he stands for something, because he has a strong agenda that people can relate to. Even our very early polls showed that there were a number of people who thought that Reagan was a very strong leader, even though they had great doubts about where he was leading us. I think Reagan has problems this year in leadership in the White House, particularly. But the fact is that Reagan has always managed to project some kind of image of leadership and to understand that this is related to the way one governs.

Reagan knows about overexposure. That is one reason that he limits not only his press conferences, but carefully picks his speeches and the spots where he is televised. Reagan understands that there is a different impact when you see something than when you hear or read it. For example, Ronald Reagan signed, as governor of California, the most permissive abortion bill in the history of the United States; when he appears with his right-to-life friends, he does not appear with them on the same platform. He addresses them electronically so that what you see is the voice-over of the commentator describing what Ronald Reagan has said. That has a different sort of impact.

When a tape is taken of him when he is doing a speech or a debate or something, Ronald Reagan will sometimes say, "That wasn't right, let's do it again." He has a sense, in other words, of what he is doing and why he is doing it. That's very important to his success, but it isn't the reason for his success.

Now let's take the gaffes and the one-liners: They've given those of us who cover the White House regularly something to look forward to. Reagan will say these wonderful things. During the first term, they had what they call the "Deaver rule," named after Mike Deaver. The rule came about because Reagan would answer questions during picture-taking sessions, which they call photo opportunities. I have never seen this described in precisely the right way, so permit me to do it. The problem with Reagan is not that he doesn't want to answer questions; the problem with Reagan is that he does. He loves to answer questions; he wants to answer your question, and wants to answer every reporter's question. He is a courteous person and he wants to answer the question whether or not he has the information with which to answer it. This is the source of the problem. So Mike thought of this rule. He hated it to be called the Deaver rule, and knowing that, we all called it that. The notion was that when you would go in to take a picture of the President when he is sitting there with the prime minister of the Republic of Ishmingle, you would not then pounce upon the President and say, "What do you think about Tip O'Neill yesterday saying you were an idiot, Mr. President?" or "How are you going to handle the problem of INF?" which then poses the problem that he's got to know what INF is. He's got to know what the reporter has in his mind. He's got to respond to the question.

So very early in the presidency, in something that is really a neglected chapter for those who investigate communications, the television correspondents at the White House all said, "We're going to ask the President what we want to ask him, just as we did with other presidents." Other presidents would just say, "No comment. I won't answer your questions." I saw Carter during a session where he looked as if he were the prisoner of war. Carter was an especially uncommunicative prisoner of war. Reagan could be too, but he isn't willing to do it. The correspondents were very tough about this, but not one of their bureaus backed them up. You see, the threat was that you wouldn't get in to get your pictures if you persisted in asking questions on other subjects, and television lives by pictures. So the Deaver rule applied. But Reagan, thank God, would sometimes forget the Deaver rule or ignore it. He always ignored it if there was something he wanted to say. He was supposed to say, "I don't take questions at photo opportunities," but one day he absentmindedly said, "I don't take questions at news conferences."

Last week at Grenada, Sam Donaldson confronted Reagan, who was "Speakes-less" and in need of him, and said, "You are here at the scene of your greatest military adventure. How does it feel to be here?" Reagan said, "I didn't fire a shot." Good answer, I thought. I thought it was one of the best answers I ever heard a president or a politician give in any circumstance. It was self-deprecating; it was saying, "Look, we lost 19 people here." There were 45 killed in Grenada; the Cubans lost more than 50.

Reagan is often accused of being cinematic, but he knows the difference between real gore and the make-believe kind. That's what that answer indicated. Almost any other answer would have gotten him in trouble, I think. He might have said how wonderful it was to be in Grenada, which we liberated. He didn't do that.

I have only one criteria for a Reaganism: It should be evocative, and if it makes people laugh, that's good too. I don't care whether it makes Reagan look good or look bad; none of that bothers me. I get people sometimes who say, "Why do you use those lines about the President?" I say, "You look back at them and you will find that a number of those lines served the purposes of the Great Communicator well." Why did they serve his purpose? Because they make him seem like one of us. He talks in ordinary people terms, he makes jokes about himself, he puts himself down. Those of you who, like I, were raised in a family of Democrats knew that it was the Democratic party, not the Democrat party, the way the Republicans always said it. Watch Ronald Reagan; he says the Democratic party. He was one of us too. The real effectiveness of rhetoric is to be able to put yourself in the shoes of the person to whom you are speaking and to elevate, uplift, reach, or move him. Reagan is truly the Great Communicator.

Having said that, I still think he is in for a tough year. And one of these years I'm going to be right.

QUESTION: A couple of weeks back President Reagan had an interesting response when he was asked a hypothetical question: "What would you do if . . . , Mr. President?" He responded, "I don't answer 'what if' questions." He said he got that from Franklin Roosevelt. Do you think that is a good policy for him to keep to?

MR. CANNON: I think he actually said, "I don't answer 'if' questions." I think he attributed that to Franklin Roosevelt. A lot of Reagan's answers—and a lot of our answers, too, I suppose—are right for the first two sentences; it is the third sentence that gets him into trouble. He says that Roosevelt never departed from that, which of course is not true. The question was: "Is it good for Reagan to do this?" I think that Reagan's response was a kind of rhetorical embellishment. No one likes to answer hypothetical questions; I think Reagan is well advised not to. If you look at the hypothetical questions he does answer, you wind up in the jungles of Central America or somewhere where neither he nor we want to be. But, like other people who have said that, he answers hypothetical questions when it suits his purpose. While no immediate examples spring to mind, there are several occasions where Reagan has in fact taken a hypothetical question and answered it.

A lot of times in foreign policy it is necessary for any President to take that view. For example, "What if Gadhafi has a terrorist attack in America; what would you do?" That is the kind of question that you are not supposed to answer, it seems to me, from the presidential podium.

QUESTION: What will be the effect of the *Challenger* space shuttle disaster on Mr. Reagan?

MR. CANNON: Judging from what we know now, which appears to be that people ignored warnings from this company and launched when they shouldn't have, it seems to me that this is not going to come back particularly as a White House problem. The administration did something that I think was very wise, although at first I wasn't sure how wise it was. You remember their first idea was that NASA was going to investigate itself, but then the White House appointed a commission. They did it, I think, not because they thought anything was wrong, but because they thought that the first plan might give the appearance of impropriety. Now I think it's very good that they've done it.

I think the problem is not going to be that the White House or the administration will be particularly blamed for this tragedy, which happens in bureaucracies. I think that the extent of the problem is going to make it much more difficult than anybody originally thought for one who favors the manned space program, as the President does, to get it going again. I think that there will be a real concern, probably in 1987, when we are scheduling launches again, about whether we are protecting the people who are going to go on those launches. It seems to me that that's where the administration is going to have some difficult decisions to make. I think the President is going to be pressing very, very strongly for continuation of the manned space flight program, despite what this inquiry has shown. My guess is that he will be able to get public and congressional support for that.

QUESTION: What important changes would you say there are in the second Reagan term in his relationship with some of his staff, especially Weinberger, Regan, Casey, and Shultz?

MR. CANNON: I see a very important change occurring in the Reagan administration in this term. The first term is an illustration of why presidencies are really run by people who are not the sum of a bunch of organization charts. If you were to describe the way the White House worked in the first term, and I did, it sounds like you are describing a pattern that is totally chaotic. You had Baker and Meese and Deaver and Stockman pitted off against Regan, and Stockman pitted off against Weinberger, and the White House staff pitted off against Haig, and Haig thinking that everybody was out to get him. And they were, not realizing that he was one of those who was out to get them. You had this sort of absolute frenzy. It was very good for the presidency and very good for this President, and therefore good for the country, because there were all sorts of viewpoints and ideas that were brought to the attention of Ronald Reagan.

Helen Caldecott, the peace activist, spent two hours one day in the office with Regan because Maureen or Patti or somebody—I think it was Maureen—thought it was a good idea and called Deaver and Deaver arranged it. Mike Deaver, who was not a substantive person in terms of any given policy, was very good in terms of Reagan because he knew that Reagan needed to be exposed to a whole range of ideas.

Pat Buchanan told me that when he went to the White House, he had a lot of ideas about what his role would be that didn't turn out to be true. He contrasted for me the preparing of Reagan for a press conference with the preparing of Nixon, who wanted everything on paper. Nixon wanted all of his stuff prepared for him. He had a tremendous command of facts, and he wanted it all funneled through one or two people who would come and help him with this preparation. Reagan assembled 13 people in the family theater, said Buchanan. It was crazy. Everybody was asking this question and that and standing up and putting an idea to him. That's the way Ronald Reagan learns. Ronald Reagan does not learn from briefing papers; he doesn't have a command of facts that Nixon or Carter have, but he has a much better people sense than either of them have.

Now he has a nice, corporate, hierarchical structure in which everything comes funneled to him through Donald Regan. I think that is not good for Reagan. Apart from the substance of Regan's ideas, I think that Regan does present different sides; I think he is an honest broker, but everything is distilled. Reagan's model was that of FDR who insisted on having all of these viewpoints from all sides. Reagan had a lot of that in his first term; he has much less of it now. Stockman was an independent force. Jim Miller is not; he is basically a regulator. He is a good guy, but he does not have a powerful command of the budget in mathematical terms that Stockman did.

So you are down to a very small selection of advisers: Cap Weinberger is more rigid than he was, in my view. I would question whether Reagan is getting the broad range of opinions in some things that he needs. I think that that's a problem for him, although not an insurmountable problem. He's got Shultz and other people with ideas around him, but it is much more constricted than it was in the first term.

QUESTION: Concerning the Reagan administration's tendency for more realism in foreign policy, could you expand on that in relation to Central America? And secondly, can you tell what his chances of giving additional funding to the contras are?

MR. CANNON: Next to arms control, I think Central America is the question that interests me the most in this administration. I said that the domestic issue about which I thought Reagan was most ideological was taxes. The foreign policy issue in which I think he is most ideological is Nicaragua. The problem of understanding Reagan's views on it is that people who either applaud or detract from him tend to talk about Reagan's anticommunism as if he had a uniform approach; in fact, he doesn't. He is much more pragmatic in dealing with the Soviet Union on superpower questions than he is on Central America. Reagan clearly feels that there is a very big difference between communism in Asia or in Africa and communism in Central America.

Ronald Reagan would have been able to get us out of Vietnam much more readily than President Nixon did, but he really is concerned with the dilemma posed by one of his aides who said that while we don't want another Vietnam in Central America, we also don't want another Cuba.

I argue that Reagan's defense budget is imperiled by his success in convincing people that we are spending so much more in defense. I think his Nicaragua policy is imperiled by the success of his El Salvador policy. The fact is that Duarte is doing a good job; Duarte is a guy that any liberal Democrat in this country would have been happy to have brought to power in Nicaragua. The real reason, the real concern, the real cutting edge of our involvement in Central America was the concern about what would happen in El Salvador. That is not a very big concern now. As a result, it is going to be very hard, I think, to persuade the Congress to do more for the contras. I'm persuaded by what I have seen and been told that the contras are in very bad shape militarily. I think that you are going to see a much more confrontational approach in Central America this year. Even while you compromise on other issues, I think that the Republican leadership in the House—Trent Lott, Dick

Cheney, even Bob Michel—are going to insist that there be some kind of up or down vote on military aid, because the contras can't make it on the humanitarian aid. The Republicans argue that you are getting the Democrats off the hook; they can say they have done something, while in fact they are not doing anything. I think that there will be a vote and that Reagan will lose the first round. However, Reagan is persistent, and I think he will come back. I think probably in the fall you will get something for the contras, but militarily they are nowhere. It is hard for me to see how this administration could get enough aid to make them the kind of effective harassment that the President envisions them to be. I think his policy is a loser on that issue, but I don't think he is going to give it up easily.

QUESTION: You said that you were giving speeches last year at this time about Reagan at the crossroads. How much erosion of his support in Congress have you seen over the last year?

MR. CANNON: I think Reagan is better off on some issues in Congress than he was. I think probably Reagan is ahead of the game on certain kinds of foreign policy issues. Whether the Geneva summit was the great success some have depicted it as being, or just sound and fury signifying nothing, we are not going to know until the next summit, or maybe not until the summit after that. I think that Reagan does have bipartisan support for some kind of framework for arms control. I think there is a real chance for a medium-range missile agreement this year. I think he has more support in Congress than he had a year ago at this time, because most people didn't think the summit would ever come off.

Where I think he has lost support is on the tax issue. I think that more and more Republicans have looked at the alternatives facing them. They are up for election this year—at least 20 of them in the Senate, all of them in the House—and most of them simply do not want to face the choice of being depicted as being soft on defense because they are cutting defense or having to cut favorite domestic programs. They really want some kind of tax increase as a way out. I think that unless Reagan grasps how important this is to his party, he faces a very difficult time in the fall because these guys can't go out there and campaign very effectively on "I fought to get this bill through that the President vetoed and which we couldn't override." That's not much of a platform.

I think the Congress, particularly the Republican leadership in the Senate, is very upset and concerned and worried. They thought at this time last year that Reagan would, in their terms, see the light, but he hasn't. I don't think that has much to do with whether it is the fifth or sixth year other than the fact that this is the year when, if you are a Republican, you have to figure out a strategy to run with Reagan and away from him at the same time.

Reagan went to Missouri the other week. In the protectionist climate that exists there, he spoke for free trade before 800 partisan Republicans; as they say, you could hear a pin drop.

QUESTION: Have you a comment on his apparent loss in capability to bring peace in the Middle East?

MR. CANNON: I think that in the Middle East the administration's hopes were always kind of an illusion. I think we were counting almost entirely on getting King Hussein to lever Arafat and there just wasn't the leverage there. Many of the policymakers at State were telling us, even as the President was saying that his Middle East peace plan was alive, that it really wasn't. I think the administration has done poorly in that area, but I'm not sure what it is that they could do to succeed. I also have a feeling that Lebanon had a lasting psychological impact on this administration. I don't detect a kind of burning desire on this issue like I do on the issues of Central America or arms control or Third World economic problems. I don't detect that this administration really believes that there is going to be any real progress in the Middle East. It seems to me that they are just getting by, that if you were to ask what the secret hope of the administration is in the Middle East, they would say that the policy won't be any worse there when they leave. That may be very unfair, but I don't sense that it is high on anybody's agenda.

There is one objective clue. Reagan very much wanted the arms package for Jordan—not so much because he thinks the arms package for Jordan is essential, but because he made a promise to Hussein and Reagan takes his promises seriously. They all talked Reagan out of that, and he withdrew the proposal. Now if you are going to try to talk Reagan out of contra aid, you are not going to be able to succeed. But they didn't have to talk very hard on Jordan. I just don't think there is much of a policy there.

QUESTION: Would you comment on the contrast between the images of Carter and Reagan? To what extent do you see that coming through the simple, personal relationship of the President?

MR. CANNON: That's a very good question. Let me try. First of all, I guess I would have to tell you that I think there is something valid about popular images. You could make a good case that Carter didn't flip-flop on a number of things; and you can make a case, as I've made here today, that Reagan is not Teflon as Pat Schroeder, who coined that term, uses the word. Nonetheless, I think that these images convey a certain kind of symbolic truth. Carter did waffle on some critical issues in his presidency, and in his campaign for that matter, which made people think of him in that way.

There are a number of things which Reagan has done that you would think would have sunk other politicians but which haven't sunk him. My nomination is the Lebanon adventure. I've used this illustration before, and it probably applies. Stu Spencer, who is Reagan's adviser and friend, was working for Ford in 1976 when Bob Teeter, the Republican pollster, joined the campaign. They were out to beat Reagan and they did, but not without some cost. Stu said to Teeter, "Let me tell you a couple of things about this guy, Bob." The second thing that he said about him was, "He can walk away from something that no other politician could survive." I think he was right. But having said that, we oversimplify—I mean, we in the press oversimplify. We do that because we don't have enough space or enough time or enough imagination or enough brains; I oversimplify too. I think we oversimplify too much about Reagan. But yes, both of those caricatures, in my view, have meaning.

QUESTION: You mentioned how concerned the President is with his television image. I was a little curious as to whether you feel there is a big contrast between his concern for that and his concern for his image in the print media. Does he really get mad about the way he is sometimes portrayed in the print media?

MR. CANNON: Reagan gets upset about being ridiculed.   He doesn't like to be ridiculed.   As far as I know, ridicule will bother him, and any criticism of Nancy will bother him even more.   He doesn't get particularly upset about a policy criticism on television or in print.   You can hammer his policy and he is apt to sit back and say, "Well, the Democrats are having their day at it," or "That's Cannon writing again," or something like that.   If somebody is putting him down personally he doesn't like it.   As long as you keep it on a policy level he is fine.

Is he as sensitive to things in the print media? I think yes and no. He does read the morning papers, and he gets a digest of them. I have seen those digests and they give him more than the good news.   But I think he is a creature of the television age; he understands that a gaffe on television or a negative portrayal on television has more impact.   In other words, I don't think that he personally makes the distinction other than as a realistic political distinction.   It is much worse to screw up on television than to do it in an interview with the *Washington Post*.

QUESTION: How much influence do you think Reagan will have over the 1988 presidential race?

MR. CANNON: I think that Reagan will not have much influence in the 1988 presidential race at all if you refer to selecting candidates.   But in terms of his economic policies of the last year, whether we have tight money or not—on which he has got to get a little help from the Federal Reserve Board—and on what assignments he gives his vice president, he can have a lot of indirect impact.   His policies could have an enormous impact.   One of the great things about our system is that "I like Ike" didn't work as a slogan.   It worked for Ike but it didn't work for the people who disliked him and who were Republicans.   Roosevelt went out in 1938 to purge eight Democratic senators who had opposed his policy.   He was "0 for Eight."   Ronald Reagan cannot anoint his successor.

QUESTION: In reference to the Supreme Court and its decision concerning Gramm-Rudman-Hollings: How will that impact on Reagan's absolutely intense hatred of a tax increase? Do you think he will see the light if we can't balance the budget over the long term?

MR. CANNON: It is dangerous to predict what any court will do, as any lawyer knows. I'm not a lawyer, but I know that much. I think the court is probably going to uphold the lower court decision, which simply has the effect of removing an automatic trigger. If the Court upholds the decision it is going to help Reagan. The real worry that the people in the White House have is that Congress will go home and this automatic something they call the "sequester" would make all these defense budget cuts. Without that provision, I think it is going to have to be negotiated. I would say it isn't going to affect Reagan's basic feeling about taxes, but it means that Reagan is going to negotiate without having a gun at his head. I think he has the high ground. I think that the Court will have given Reagan an advantage over the Democrats.

QUESTION: Two distinguishing Reagan policies in the international arena seem to be an uncompromising belief in the Strategic Defense Initiative and an almost uncompromising opposition to the Sandinistas in Nicaragua. In a previous answer you suggested that Mr. Reagan is not quite at the crossroads yet on matters of Nicaragua. Is he pushing the crossroads on matters of SDI?

MR. CANNON: That's a really good question, the answer to which my editors would like me to find out. Let me make what we used to call on the police beat a confession: I don't know. I think that Reagan has a little running room on SDI. It is interesting that the Soviets have dropped their insistence that the United States stop research and development of weapons in space, what they call space strike weapons, which is somewhat broader than SDI but includes SDI, as a condition of negotiation on other types of arms control. The Soviets know we are going to continue with research on that. They are researching on it, too. SDI has succeeded, even if one doesn't think it is feasible or like the idea, in getting the Soviets to where they are now. At some point, it seems to me, the President is going to have to compromise—not scrap it, but say we will agree not to deploy A, B, and C—and we will confine our research to those areas.

Gorbachev has made it easy on him. He has not said what would be an acceptable limit. In the *Time* interview he said research is fine; other times he has been as imprecise as Reagan, seeming to suggest that we cease it entirely.

I think that if they are able to get through some kind of an interim agreement limiting medium-range weapons in Europe, Gorbachev would be in a position to say before the Moscow summit in 1987, "We've gone (a Reagan phrase) the extra mile on this and now you have to make some concessions." I'm not a Soviet expert, but if he has the creativity and flexibility and the support of his system to be able to do that, then my guess is that Reagan will run into that particular wall, not in the sixth year but in the seventh, in which case I can go somewhere else and give the speech, "Reagan at the Crossroads."

NARRATOR: All of us, I think, will look forward to the next Lou Cannon Rotunda lecture when we look a year from now at Reagan at the Crossroads. We thank you most sincerely.

CHAPTER 7

WILL THERE BE A REAGAN LEGACY?

SANDER VANOCUR

NARRATOR: Teaching for most people (except television preachers) is not a matter of hamming it up, but of having one, two or three good students. I had three at Northwestern, but Sandy was by far the most outstanding, and all the other faculty had the same view. Sandy went on for postgraduate work at London, and he began his media career writing for the Manchester *Guardian*. He then had a whole succession of appointments: to the city staff of the *New York Times*, as British correspondent of CBS News, and then for NBC News from 1957 to 1971. He was on the "Today Show" and then host for the "First Tuesday" TV show. He was White House correspondent and then senior correspondent of National Public Affairs Center for TV (a division of Public Broadcasting Service). He was a TV columnist for the *Washington Post*, vice president for special reporting units of ABC News and Sports, and chief diplomatic correspondent.

Sandy is currently doing a program on business that even University faculty could learn something from. It is a professional and personal privilege to welcome Sandy Vanocur again to the University of Virginia.

MR. VANOCUR: As Ken says, I cover business now. I had been covering politics for many years, but I decided I couldn't go out and cover politics any more and stay in one more Quality Court Motel. Once Barbara Walters asked George Burns if he thought much about death, and he replied, "No." Then she asked why and he said, "It's been done." I decided I wanted to cover business for a similar

139

reason. I have covered two epic stories in my life before: the story of civil rights in the South in the late 1950s and early 1960s, and the war in Vietnam, both in Vietnam and the reaction to the war here at home. Now the big question seems to be whether America can maintain its economic vitality—not the dominance it had, but the economic vitality that it had—for the rest of the century. This might prove to be another of the big epic stories.

Since I decided to start covering business, I have found that my experience in Washington has been quite valuable to me. I believe that I came at the right time, too, because we are now seeing the final harvest of Reaganomics, which I judge to have been a failure, but not for the reasons that a lot of people think. Reaganomics can be misleading because if you look at it—at least the record by the end of 1988—it appears to be a huge statistical success. Reagan now has presided over the longest peacetime expansion in post-World War II history; inflation is down from 12.4 percent in 1980 to less than 5 percent this year (though there are some worries that it may be nudging back a little higher than 5 percent). Some people say that Paul Volcker, as chairman of the Federal Reserve Board, deserves the credit for this, and that is possibly true. If so, though, he also has to take the blame for shoving us into the terrible recession in 1982 to accomplish this. If we had high inflation now, Ronald Reagan would be blamed for it; but since we don't have it, I think Ronald Reagan should be given credit for avoiding it. The misery index, that rough measure of popular discontent that is formed by summing the rates of inflation and unemployment, is down dramatically from 19.5 percent in 1980 to less than 10 percent right now; 15 million new jobs have been created; and individual taxes are down from 70 to 28 percent (even though it takes a super computer to compute one's taxes under the new tax simplification guidelines).

On the minus side we have record budget deficits. We have also had record trade deficits under Reagan, though I must say I'm not sure it would be any different on that score if a Democrat were president. We've gone from being the world's largest creditor nation to being the world's largest debtor nation. Yet I think when Reagan leaves next January, barring any unforeseen revelations by White House aides, he will leave office a very beloved President.

Now how did he pull this off? I think he did it because, as his one-time political campaign manager, John Sears, once so brilliantly put it, "Ronald Reagan treats reality as an illusion that can be overcome." Reagan also began office with one advantage. He is the first president to take office since the death of John F. Kennedy who didn't seem preoccupied or fearful that a Kennedy, first Robert and then Edward, would make a claim to the seals of the office that had been stripped from their older brother at the hand of an assassin. All presidents in varying degrees since the death of John F. Kennedy have been seized with this preoccupation. Probably the least preoccupied with the Kennedys before Reagan was Jerry Ford.

I had some early moments of doubt when Reagan took office about how he was going to pull all this off. During the inaugural gala in 1981 Rich Little was doing an impression of Ronald Reagan interviewed by Walter Cronkite. The interview went like this. Cronkite: "Mr. President, you promised the American people you would substantially increase the defense budget and reduce the deficit at the same time you cut taxes. How are you going to do it?" Reagan: "We'll keep two sets of books."

A key Reagan promise from the beginning was to get government off the backs of the people. Now why I think this has been a failure is that it goes against all American experience since 1933. The crash of 1929, the bank failures that followed in the 1930s, and the Depression that followed those two events did more than make millions of Americans poor and unemployed; it shattered, though it didn't totally destroy, the idea of free markets. Then the New Deal introduced, though in a very chaotic and haphazard way, the idea that an activist federal government must intervene in the market economy in a variety of ways to make sure that capitalism didn't fail. Thus the idea that government must play a major role in our economic planning has been accepted by every president, Republican and Democrat, until Reagan took office. But Reagan, the man who treats reality as an illusion that can be overcome, was able to succeed at the outset. He really is a political magician. He is able to appeal to one of our more fascinating but troubling national characteristics, which is our ability to hold two conflicting ideas in our mind at the same time and believe both of them.

We Americans are against every known government program, except all those from which we personally benefit. Our election results since 1952 bear this out. In that time Republican presidents, promising to reduce the functions and size and the cost of federal government, have occupied the White House for a total of 24 years. During the same period the Democrats have occupied the White House for 12 years, and just barely managed to gain it in 1976 when Carter ran against Ford. Since 1952, though, the Republicans have controlled the House of Representatives for only two years and the Senate for only six, those six being those that have just gone by in this decade.

What is the moral of this? I think it is that we hedge our bets. We elect Republican presidents who promise thrift, but for the most part Democratic Congresses who continue to give us all the programs that we think are too costly. More importantly, this voting behavior suggests, by and large, that when it comes to delivering all those programs, which the Reagan revolution has cited as being too costly, the American people perceive the Democratic delivery system as Federal Express and the Republican delivery system as the pony express. I don't think this is going to change either, because I don't think any president from here to the end of the century is going to be able to shape the American political scene as Reagan did during his first four years in office, as FDR did from 1933 to 1937, or as Johnson did from 1965 to 1967.

I think the reason for this is that we have short memories in this country; we forget that there is precedent for this. Indeed, the New Deal ran out of steam in 1937 when Roosevelt suffered some political setbacks, including his scheme to pack the Supreme Court. We were pulled out of the Depression by World War II, which made us the dominant economic force in the world for the next 40 years. The Reagan revolution ran out of steam as well. A part of the reason for this, I think, is the genius of the Founding Fathers in making our system one of countervailing forces. I also think that presidents suffer from hubris: Roosevelt's packing of the Supreme Court proved that he was mortal; Lyndon Johnson getting us involved as deeply as he did in Vietnam followed up what Kennedy and Eisenhower had done before to a much more limited degree. Reagan likewise made a terrible mistake in 1985. He took on the Congress of the United States on two of the worst issues he could have possibly chosen, water and highways, and he got beaten badly on both. That was the end of presidential immortality as far as he was concerned.

Something else was also happening at that time that was not too well observed, but which I think was terribly important. The boll weevils in the House of Representatives, those Southern Democrats who voted with Republicans to get Reagan's legislation through, were returning to the fold for a number of complex reasons. One was the fact that the House Democratic leadership was providing the kind of leadership that would allow these Southern Democrats to be able to sell their programs back home. One illustration of how badly the coalition had fallen apart, how badly the administration had judged the support of Southern Democrats, was the Bork nomination. The South just was not there then for Ronald Reagan in terms of Democratic senators.

More striking than that was the victory of Congressman Wyche Fowler in Georgia over the Republican incumbent, Mack Mattingly, for the Senate in 1986. Fowler was an Atlanta liberal, but he carried 109 of the state's 159 counties, including rural counties where no liberal was ever supposed to win. He campaigned in those counties by going directly against the dream of the Reagan revolution, by talking about the need for government to spend more money on education and economic development. To me, if ever there was a sign the Reagan revolution was over, it came in those southern Georgia rural counties in 1986.

Now, if these patterns hold, and I think they are going to, the next president, whether he be George Bush or Michael Dukakis, is going to face an era of congressional government, the kind of government that Woodrow Wilson warned about in his famous book in 1896. That is a government where the Congress, if not coequal, at least will not be subservient to the president and will not be rolled over by strong presidents, as a lot of our Congresses have been for the past 30 or 40 years. One of the main reasons for this is that there is now in the Congress of the United States, and especially in the House, the closest thing in politics to academic tenure. This is another example of a law of unintended consequences; it is the result of political action committees, which can virtually guarantee incumbents, especially those with seniority or those with terribly important committee assignments and chairmanships, their political tenure through contributions.

Here is a striking statistic. In 1986 when 391 incumbents were running for reelection, only seven challengers to them were successful. And this year *Congressional Quarterly* estimates that in six states accounting for one-third of the House membership—Texas, California, Pennsylvania, Ohio, Florida, and New Jersey—there are about ten challenges to incumbents that are deemed significant. I don't know if this is good or bad, but I do think it may match the mood of the country.

Moreover, I have a hunch that the electorate, after earlier promises of the Reagan revolution, may now want some presidential leadership that is more collegial with Congress, more managerial than inspirational, more cooperative than confrontational. People may be tired of the FDR and Reagan kind of leadership, which is throwing a bunch of balls in the air and hoping that you can catch a few while people do not see the others that fall to the ground. This is one of the reasons why the "lack of charisma" charge that has been leveled against Dukakis will not hold; people love Ronald Reagan very much, but they have had enough of charisma and now they want competence.

Rather than look at the candidates, though, I'd like to look at the parties, because I think there are still some deep divisions within the Republican party. Despite concern on the part of some Democrats about Jesse Jackson, I think the concerns should be deeper among Republicans about their party. Political parties are like primitive tribes, and they have their rituals. They have gods to whom they pay homage, and they are possessed of the necessity from time to time to appease the fury of the gods—real or imagined—by offering sacrifices. The only two sacrifices I can see on the Republican side would be the chief of staff, Howard Baker, or James Baker, who either will be running George Bush's campaign from campaign headquarters this summer or from the Treasury, where he will be battling Alan Greenspan to keep interest rates down so George Bush can ride this prosperity to victory. The charge against both of them is that they have not let Reagan be Reagan, that they have made him more pragmatic than ideological in his last two years.

All of this masks the fact that in Detroit in 1980 the Republican party achieved a measure of harmony and unity that it hadn't had since the party nominated Wendell Willkie in Philadelphia in 1940. Remember that 12 years later in Chicago, Everett Dirksen turned and pointed to Tom Dewey and said, "You took us down the road to defeat twice." Dirksen meant that the Eastern establishment had caused defeat, and he was not going to let it happen again.

The party was relatively settled but unhappy from 1960 to 1976 because Nelson Rockefeller filled a role of putative sacrifice for Republicans who believed that starting with Willkie and continuing through Eisenhower, the Eastern establishment was taking the party down the wrong historical road. Rockefeller was politically dead after 1976. Given Reagan's genial political personality and the fact that he was a Westerner, which is terribly important, factionalism was at least put on the back burner in 1980. But I believe that factionalism is awake again, and I think it is going to be manifest in the right wing of the Republican party in New Orleans during the writing of the platform. The right wing had absolutely no influence on the choice of a nominee this year, and it hurts that group.

There is perhaps a broader problem as well. Despite the efforts of Bill Brock (in the late 1970s) and Frank Fahrenkopf (from 1982 to the present time) to modernize the Republican party both in practice and in outlook, and to broaden its base, it still has a more specialized appeal than the Democratic party. The Republicans will tell you in their private moments that there is something not quite right about the image they are projecting in their effort to try to become the majority party. I have a quotation that expresses this in the best way I have ever heard:

> The problem is the Republican party has not articulated an inclusive vision of the public good that reflects concern for the well-being of the whole community. During the past half century or so Republican spokesmen have consistently emphasized private concerns such as self-discipline [and] self-reliance and either do not have or have not communicated a persuasive conception of the public good. It has been left to the Democratic party to make clear that in a civilized society, people must look out for one another and devise, however ineptly, the mechanisms for doing so.

These words came from a 1979 article in the Republican National Committee's excellent publication, *Common Sense*. The author was a Democrat who, fed up with the Democratic party views on national security, but being brought up in the political and social tradition of Scoop Jackson and Hubert Humphrey, couldn't quite join up with the Republicans at that time. The article was called

"Why We Can't Vote Republican," and the person who wrote it was Jeane Kirkpatrick. I still think the words apply today, and I bet she'd say the same thing.

I've also been fascinated by some signals being sent at least on the Democratic side, though we haven't had many because the Republican race was so short. There are some good signals coming out from polling being done, both among the swing voters and Democrats, that suggest the country is in pretty good shape, but with some concerns that are important. I think the country didn't respond to Jesse Jackson's charge about slave labor conditions overseas beating our products; the defeat of Gephardt was, I think, an endorsement for the idea of free trade and a rejection of protectionism.

Still, there is something I have been troubled with for about two years. I've not been able to put my finger on it precisely, but for want of a better phrase, I've been calling it "middle-class populism." Populism is our only enduring political philosophy, broad enough in our history to embrace everything from agrarian reform to pre–World War II isolationism to anti-Semitism. As a working reporter, I saw its first manifestations in three presidential primaries in 1964, when George Wallace successfully told voters to send Washington a message. My own common sense and a little familiarity with the South suggested to me that his appeal was based on more than racism, that George Wallace was tapping some common feeling in blue collar people in the North as well. But the blue collar populism and the middle-class populism I now see are quite different. There is a general sense on the part of people, particularly post–World War II baby boom children now approaching the lower levels of middle age, that they are not going to enjoy the same standard of living their parents enjoyed.

William Galston, who is the director of economic and social programs at the Roosevelt Center for American Policy Studies in Washington, is cited in the 2 April 1988 edition of the *National Journal*. He had been conducting so-called focus groups in February in Illinois and was shocked at what he called "this middle-class squeeze among people who have middle-class standards of living, which they fear, no matter how hard they work, they may lose." He said, "This is a persuasive fear among Democrats," and he continued, "It is particularly strong among swing Democrats—people in Illinois who voted for Reagan for President and Paul Simon for Senate in 1984." In his own report Galston says the following:

> Swing Democrats who voted for Paul Simon and Reagan in 1984, represent a middle class that feels economically and culturally besieged. They see prices for the basics of middle-class life, in particular home ownership and higher education, soaring out of sight, and to a greater extent than other groups. They see the weakening of family, community, and the work ethic as the root of many of our economic and social problems. While they see government as a tax collector rather than a benefactor, the sentiment does not resolve in a generalized tax revolt as it did during the 1970s, but rather in a rising demand for new government assistance, targeted to the hard-pressed middle class. Their intuitive belief in individual initiative and responsibility now appears to have been counterbalanced by the rising conviction that average Americans cannot deal with all their own problems on their own.

On another occasion, Galston has pointed out further that candidates are gradually stumbling into what he calls "marginality," and they are trying to figure out how to address it.

Having said that, I think that the November election is not going to be a judgment on the Reagan revolution. I think that voters, and especially the middle class, will be addressing the future in the same way voters in 1960 were. They were not casting a judgment on the administration of another popular Republican President, our last one to finish two terms in office, Dwight D. Eisenhower. Rather, they were looking to the future as defined by our first post-World War II generation nominees, Kennedy and Nixon. It is not going to be a campaign like 1980 when Ronald Reagan succeeded by defining government as the problem and not the solution. It is going to be a election about competence. Thank you.

NARRATOR: We thought it would be interesting, and in keeping with some of the previous forums, if we had two well-informed commentators, who have previously discussed politics at the Miller

Center, briefly give their views. One is Staige Blackford, the editor of the *Virginia Quarterly Review*. He is the author of the first Miller Center Commission Report on the presidential press conference. He was Governor Holton's press secretary until he descended to academia. The second is Jim Latimer, the dean of the commentators and columnists on politics in the state of Virginia. His writings on governors in the state and in broadcasts on their role have evoked much admiration and respect, and he continues to work in this area. He hasn't been at the Center for a little while, so we thought it was high time we tried to get him back. He will be the second commentator.

MR. BLACKFORD: Since you ended up talking about the forthcoming election, which is on everybody's mind, let me ask you whether you see this 1988 election as being what Arthur Schlesinger calls a "bellwether" election? Will this one be a real changeover, say like in 1932 or 1952?

MR. VANOCUR: I hate to go against that theory, which Arthur's father actually devised, because it may be fine. However, I just turned 60, and in addition to being unable to remember whom I've just called when I dial a phone, I'm getting suspicious of all generalizations, such as, "This is the end of an era." I've come to feel that if you see one end of an era, you've seen them all. I don't think it is going to be that.

I think it is going to be, for want of a better phrase, a staging area, a quiet staging area for the next political development in this country. This staging area is a lot more complicated than any I have ever seen before, largely because of the emergence of new ethnic groups. There is not only the emergence of the black vote as a powerful new bloc, but also the rising prominence of a larger group in many ways, the Hispanic vote. (I know that lumping together many Spanish-speaking groups under the label "Hispanic" is like saying Norwegians and Italians are Europeans. There are at least three components, Puerto Ricans, Cubans, and Mexican-Americans, who each have somewhat differing goals.) Finally, there are our Asian immigrants and Asian-Americans. In short, tremendous demographic changes are taking place.

In one sense, it is going to be a confirmation of one thing Reagan did do, which was to rearrange the whole rhetoric and terms of American political discussion. You are not going to see any Democrats get elected by promising more liberalism. That's not going to happen. Yet I don't see this campaign as anything more than a staging operation, which may give us distant early warnings about what the politics of the next century may be like, barring an unforeseen world calamity with markets collapsing, protectionism rising, and those sorts of things. Actually, I'm glad it's not going to be a revolutionary election, because I don't think we have much sense of where the world is headed, not just in terms of the rise of Japan, but also in terms of the newly industrialized countries of South Korea, Taiwan, Hong Kong, the Philippines, and Indonesia, which even Japan worries about. Then there is the change that China is going to bring, and God knows what is going to happen in the Soviet Union. So I'm glad that it's going to be a staging operation, and I'm glad that the people who are running it are more managerial than they are inspirational, because I'd hate for somebody to take us off into the future without any kind of a road map.

MR. LATIMER: In doing some work for the 200th anniversary of Virginia's Capitol and General Assembly, one thing I noticed was that Chapter I of the Acts of the Virginia General Assembly of 1788 sets out the way Virginia should elect its presidential electors, for the districts and so forth. There I found a wonderful 18th century phrase that "every presidential elector must be a discreet and proper person." I thought, well, that sounds pretty good even for today, but perhaps I'm reminiscing too much. At that time, though, the people of Virginia went to the courthouses on the first Wednesday in January of 1789 and elected their presidential electors, not by secret ballot but by voice vote. Then the presidential electors met on the first Wednesday in February of 1789 and voted for president. They were paid ten shillings a day for their services. In short, I think that we could learn something from our early history. We may need a few more of those "discreet and proper" people around Washington and on the presidential staffs.

To return to 1988, though, Mr. Vanocur, I'm not sure I understood you when you used the phrase, "let the good times roll." Were you saying that will be enough for the Republican ticket?

MR. VANOCUR: It's not enough. It might be, but I don't think it is enough. I am not unmindful of the electoral importance of a powerful robust economy, and I think the economy will remain robust until November. Yet I have a feeling that George Bush and his running mate have to come up with a better articulation of the Republican conception of the public good, as Jeane Kirkpatrick complained.

I don't underestimate Dukakis, though, in that he does have some ideas that he is going to throw out in the campaign. Let me just offer one example. He is now struggling to come out with a balanced budget. He'd like to have that going into the election, but more important than that, it seems to me, he became governor of the first state to pass a catastrophic medical illness bill. I cannot tell you what a powerful political issue that is. Just sit and think that it is less than 25 years since Dr. Morris Fishbein in Chicago, editor of the *Journal of the American Medical Association*, was warning us about socialized medicine. You don't hear anybody talking about socialized medicine now. You hear employers talking, and I think legitimately, about the costs of medical programs, but all of us now assume the propriety of medical care for virtually everyone. One of the biggest costs items is high technology treatment, and the system is spewing out these inventions faster than we come up with ways to utilize them. That's one issue that a lot of people are thinking about. Therefore I think that the proposition of merely continuing Reagan's prosperity will not be enough for most Republicans and certainly not for most Americans.

MR. LATIMER: If Ronald Reagan could run again, and ran on his Reaganomics record, would he be reelected?

MR. VANOCUR: I think that if we did not have these unfortunate revelations, he probably could run again, but I think people would like to see him retire with honor and dignity. He also is the victim of Roosevelt, his first political hero, in that we now have a constitutional amendment limiting presidents to two terms. I'm glad he is not going to run again, for his own sake and ours.

MR. BLACKFORD: I'm fascinated by this idea of middle-class populism, partly because we almost saw something like that happen in this state in 1973 when Henry Howell ran for governor. And I'm just curious because of what else is going on—you and I are both from the South where we experienced the civil rights revolution—and there is always talk of putting working-class whites together with blacks to form a pretty powerful political alliance. Do you see any likelihood of that down the road?

MR. VANOCUR: I don't see that political alliance happening. I see more of a chance for such a political alliance in the North than in the South. The South, as Harry Ashmore used to say, can be much less hypocritical than the North about the black-white situation. According to him, the sentiment among Southern whites in the 1950s was, "Come close but don't go too high," while in the North the sentiment was "Go high but don't come too close." I think the political configurations and possibilities are different in that sense. But in the Midwest, the Rust Belt, I see a better possibility for an alliance among blue-collar workers, black and white.

It is interesting that you bring up Henry Howell, because he had enough appeal to get people interested, but not quite enough to keep them from being frightened either. What I think Dukakis will try to do with middle-class populism is to make several groups comfortable with each other, but frighten them collectively about their social status. On the other hand, he cannot be too pessimistic because he would underestimate the power of Reagan's achievement in making us feel good about ourselves again. Any Democrat who tries to go campaigning wearing a hair shirt on the outside is going to lose, so this is a very tricky thing. The alliance you are talking about between Southern blacks and white Southern workers is possible, but I think I see its manifestations further north for the moment than down here.

MR. LATIMER: A week or so ago there was a piece in the *Washington Post* by Arthur Schlesinger saying that we were due a new round of liberalism in the cycle of American politics. He wrote as if it were almost inevitable that we would now swing into a liberal cycle in the 1990s or maybe as early as this year's election. Do you see anything like that?

MR. VANOCUR: Well, there may be a return to something in the cycle, but it better not be called "liberalism," or it will be dead while it is being born. You don't ever hear people on the Hill like Tony

Coelho, who is the Majority Whip and who has been so successful in the Congressional Reelection Committee during the 1980s when the Democrats could have lost so many seats, using the word *liberalism*. This again is where Reagan has changed the terms of rhetoric in our campaign. You hear them talking about competence, efficiency, and productivity. Look at Dukakis' rhetoric; he sounds like a businessman in stressing investment and partnership. That's the approach now and that's why I am so fascinated by the new relationship between the private sector and the government. But you won't hear of "liberalism."

I don't even think the manifestations of this emerging consensus will be liberal; I think it will be pragmatic. What Arthur is trying to prove—with all respect to him—is a theory which may come about. But it will not be a neat return to the past with the old labels, and I think if the Democrats are smart they will not call it "liberalism." I don't think it is liberalism; it's pragmatism.

MR. LATIMER: I always have trouble distinguishing between populism and liberalism. Is populism just a sort of an alias for liberalism?

MR. VANOCUR: No, populism is historically far more radical than liberalism. It could be right-wing, or it could be left-wing. Out where Ken and I grew up in the Midwest, I could cite for example the book Bill Greider wrote on the Federal Reserve Board, which is an attack on Paul Volcker, the Federal Reserve Board, big banks, and so forth. When I was in Tokyo in December and interviewed Volcker, I asked him if he had read the book. He said, "Greider is a populist," and I said, "Of course he is, Paul." If you grew up in Illinois where I grew up, or in downstate Ohio where Bill grew up, that's what you would think about the Eastern banks. That's how I felt about the Cleveland Trust when I was a kid living in Cleveland! It is worse now in this age when it is easier to get your checks cashed at a liquor store than it is in a bank!

This is not so much a liberal-radical problem, I think, as it is a geographical phenomenon. Howard Phillips made a good observation when he recently said at a conservative caucus about George Bush, "All those ideas from Hanover and Yale won't work." And nothing does George Bush such harm as when he says things like: "My father, Prescott Bush, got mad at me and he wanted to punish me; I don't know whether he came at me with a lacrosse stick or a squash racquet." Those things still matter in this country. It runs all throughout our literature. Greider's is a geographical book. You shouldn't think about it in terms of liberalism or radicalism; it is geographical. At its roots, though, it is radical.

In a way, Barry Goldwater's approach was radical in 1964, but like most things in this marvelous system that we have, they've been adopted just like all of Norman Thomas's ideas have been adopted by both parties. I think it is only journalists who use these dumb phrases!

MR. BLACKFORD: You mentioned that Eisenhower was the last two-term Republican president. As you all know, he warned about the military-industrial complex, which seems to be quite a problem now. What will happen to that after Reagan?

MR. VANOCUR: I think what happens depends to a great extent on what happens in the Soviet Union. But more importantly it is what happens in many congressional districts in this country that have large defense establishments. If we came back to the term *liberal*, Alan Cranston personifies that word as much as anyone. Do you want to watch Alan's votes on defense legislation, though? They are very steadily in favor of contracts for his district. The change that the new American president has to accomplish is to have a defense policy that is not so Soviet-oriented, but is more oriented toward the kind of situation we have in the Persian Gulf. The idea of an unlimited defense budget, though, is over; it's gone, and whether he resigned for personal reasons or because he lost the battle, Caspar Weinberger did more to contribute to the abstinence of Congress, on both sides of the aisle, in refusing free checks to the military than anybody else. So I think that the military-industrial complex that Eisenhower warned about has now evolved into a general consensus. The free lunch is over for the military, and they have to account for their funds just like everybody else.

MR. LATIMER: I'd like to bring up the issue of Bush's vulnerability as a candidate. Some observers have mentioned the idea that George Bush had better get either Bob Dole or Baker on as his vice presidential candidate because there is some possibility that some revelation about the Iran-contra episode could explode and eliminate Bush as a presidential candidate. That seems pretty far-fetched to me, but do you have any opinion about the plausibility of that?

MR. VANOCUR: It has been a big year for surprises, but I have the feeling that George Bush has gotten that contra business pretty well under control. If you want to start unraveling that ball of yarn, you are going to go all the way back to Jimmy Carter and his CIA, and no administration's hands are quite clean on propping up these petty dictators. I really don't think that that's the issue he has to worry about in the choice of his vice president. I think that some of the American people have made a decision about contra aid and the use of our weapons to placate Khomeini to get hostages and so forth. He has to make a decision on the vice presidency on the basis of how that person will help him get elected. Right now that is a very tough decision, because I don't think Howard Baker wants to be his running mate, and he has to ask what person brings something to the ticket. Lamar Alexander of Tennessee would bring a great deal of confidence, enlightenment, and attractiveness. Alan Simpson of Wyoming brings the most blessed virtue, I think, which is his sense of humor, but he also only brings you Wyoming! If Deukmejian left, that would allow a Democrat to become governor, and I think it would be very confusing to have a Deukmejian here and a Dukakis there—kind of confusing in the voter's mind! Seriously, though, Bush has to take a good look at who helps him.

Bob Dole, who I thought would run a better campaign, actually hurt Jerry Ford in 1976. I thought Ford's best choice for running mate in 1976 was Anne Armstrong of Texas. I thought she would have helped Jerry Ford. It has been calculated that Robert Dole cost that ticket 2 percent and they lost the election to Carter by less than that. I really don't think that the Iran-contra investigations would hurt George Bush as much as a bad running mate would.

NARRATOR: Sandy, would it be fair to say that, in contrast to everything that was said around this table between 1980 and 1982 about the realignment within and between parties, you believe that the Reagan legacy is a change in the political environment, atmosphere, and ideas, but not a change in membership and participation in the parties?

MR. VANOCUR: Yes, and I even thought so at the time. I remember arguing, with George Will, on David Brinkley's show, who said the 1984 election represented "a permanent political realignment." I said, "If you've seen one permanent political realignment, you've seen them all." The shifting sands of American politics are difficult to understand from the surface. There are shifts, but they are very deep and hard to divine. All the things that we thought we'd see didn't take place after the "Reagan revolution."

Now one thing did occur that I think has done profound damage to the Republican party, and that is Watergate. We saw the early manifestations of that in two events: one, the election of large numbers of Democrats to the Congress in 1974, and second, Ford's loss in the 1976 election, which was largely due to his early and somewhat secretive pardon of Richard Nixon, which cost Ford the election. For the Republicans to gain control of the House, at least by the 1990s (following the 1990 census and redistricting and reapportionment), they would have had to have done well all these years in the state legislatures. According to some public opinion that I respect, the worst harm of Watergate was setting them back in their attempts starting in 1974 to reach that goal. Had that taken place, you would have seen a tangible political realignment in the sense that realignment is numbers of votes, people in the House, and so forth.

In terms of the other aspects, though, I think the whole thing is in flux; the Republicans are not going to become the majority party for as far into the future as I can see. The Democrats, I think, will be strengthened because, as I say, the impact of this immigrant vote, especially the Hispanic-American vote, is going to be just huge. Here is a statistic that I throw out that may startle you: By the year 2000 Chicago may be a predominantly Hispanic city. California, I think, figures to be 34 percent Hispanic now, and that's the fastest growing group.

QUESTION: How would you evaluate the very serious problem of the deficit as it applies to either party taking over? The deficit is going to really hogtie an urge to loosen up spending on the liberal side (I'm using that bad word). At the same time, if anybody attempts to raise taxes, he is going to push us into a recession. It's a heads-I-win, tails-you-lose proposition for whoever comes to power.

MR. VANOCUR: I agree, and the financial markets are always to be ignored because they claimed that it was the deficit that forced the October 19th crash. But as Bill Gray, the chairman of the Budget Committee, said in a memorable quote, "They weren't too concerned about Magic Kingdom economics during that period of bull markets." Now people are saying that if you push the deficit down too fast and by too much, you will throw us into a recession. I think no Democrat can go in there and raise taxes; the country doesn't want that. What a Democrat or a Republican can do is to seize upon the beneficial aspects of Gramm-Rudman-Hollings, the sense that we have to do something about the budget, not to please the financial markets, not to please foreign investors, but because it ought to be done with all deliberate speed. That is going to call for some hard choices and for reductions in what I have called "middle-class entitlements." A lot of my associates in the middle class don't think they are entitlements at all, but whatever they are, they have to be addressed.

Appointing a bipartisan Hoover Commission or something like that does not really address it. It takes government, and it is going to take cooperation on both sides of the aisle, if that can be brought about. The President and his party have to set the tone. The Democrats can't avoid this any more, though, because they are again the majority party in both houses. Actually, I think the deficit is being addressed now, and I think that is one of the beneficial things of these last few years. Though I do think Reagan's policies of raising the defense budget to the greatest heights since World War II and cutting taxes at the same time have brought this about, the Democrats are not without blame either.

QUESTION: I happened to have been involved with Frank Nash when this phrase "military-industrial-political complex" was brought up, and when Frank came back having talked to President Eisenhower, who liked what was being proposed, he left out the word "political" in his speech. The layer-caking that each special interest has *in the Congress* is what drives this thing; each trades off and nobody wants to blame the Congress. Everybody blames industry or the military, but Congress is the real cause. Take a look at agriculture. The special interests there have driven the cost of farm subsidies out of sight. My point is that when we talk about defense spending, you have to face up to what the Congress has done without regard to executive effort to try to hold the costs down.

MR. VANOCUR: I agree with you. Just to take one case, consider the problems of closing a Navy yard or a military installation. Oddly, what you have to address—and this is not as roundabout as it seems—is the deleterious effect of political reform. Political reform has ruined politics in this country. I want to go back to the system we had when Maurice Stans went around busting corporate kneecaps for Nixon in 1972. We need to take limits off spending and get rid of political action committees. So many problems in this country would be ameliorated. You will break up what has become a calcification in the Congress, but I am a voice in the wilderness about political reform.

QUESTION: Mr. Vanocur, there has been some discussion this morning, perhaps based on the writings of recent historians, about the cyclical pattern of populism. Could it be that this is wrong, and the nation is actually experiencing a return to progressivism, not dissimilar to the political mood of the 1912–16 period?

MR. VANOCUR: Yes, you are absolutely right; that's a welcome correction. I was thinking about Harold Ickes this morning, who came out of the Bull Moose school. I remember in 1964 sitting in a hotel room in Kansas City predicting to Bill Scranton that he would be in the Republican race one way or another before the summer. He said he wouldn't be. Then we digressed and I commented that I couldn't understand why a Republican didn't come along and run on either the radical Toryism of Disraeli's 19th century kind in Britain or Theodore Roosevelt's Progressivism. Today I can't understand why somebody in the Republican party doesn't come along and try that, because I think it would sweep the day; I suppose it is just not possible now, given the nature of the Republican party.

Progressivism as a trend is fine, though; it's even better than populism. Populism has some ugly ramifications because of our history. Progressivism of the Teddy Roosevelt period is just wonderful; you could dress it up with all the slogans and historical events around it and it would be perfect. It fits in our finest tradition—Robert LaFollette, etc. I'm surprised no one's exploited that favorable position.

QUESTION: You indicated that there has been a change in the public attitude towards military spending, and I think that's true. When Reagan came in, he was saying that America should stand tall and be firm with the Russians and so on, but he has clearly moderated his policies since 1985. What do you think the outlook is in the future for candidates in their attitude towards the Soviet Union?

MR. VANOCUR: Well, any candidate who runs from now on could always refer back to Ronald Reagan, whether he wanted to be tough or to be moderate. "Standing tall" as a slogan caught on because Jimmy Carter produced in his countrymen a sense of impotence about our ability to manage our affairs at home and abroad. I was astonished when Jimmy Carter, speaking to the hostage families in 1979, said that he wouldn't use force to get those hostages back. Any time the President of the United States publicly renounces the use of force, you have in effect a pacifist in the White House. I think that statement, and the ineptness of our effort to rescue the hostages in April 1980, was too much for the American people; it snapped something. After that they were willing to go along with Ronald Reagan in almost anything he wanted to do in the realm of defense.

What I think Ronald Reagan and Gorbachev have combined to do is to cease to make the Soviet Union the preoccupation of our foreign affairs for the first time since the end of World War II. Now it could also be—and I want to modify that—that the Soviet fixation will be replaced by continued preoccupation with Central America, and future historians reviewing this a hundred years from now will never understand how we could spend so much time on Central America. But it seems to me that the Soviet Union will not be the preoccupation of the next president or the president after that because there are too many other forces loose in the world that are causing our attention to be focused on other matters. These include trade, China, and the role of Japan in the world.

QUESTION: Do you think this will make it much more difficult to develop consensus in this country on foreign policy? Hammering the Soviets has been the conventional way that we have achieved consensus.

MR. VANOCUR: Yes, I think it will be more difficult and more easy at the same time. We have a whole new generation who didn't grow up with the fear of the Soviet Union that came out of World War II. Remember that one of the persons most responsible for both the exacerbation of our relations with China and the Soviet Union, and then for the improvement of those relations, has been Richard Milhous Nixon. He has had it both ways. In my adult lifetime no other figure has so dominated the political scene, in my mind, as Richard Nixon, starting when I was a freshman in 1946 at Northwestern University. If you want to chart the ebb and flow of anti-Sovietism and détente, it's all in that one man. Many other Americans didn't grow up that way because they are of a later generation, and they have other preoccupations like how they are going to pay for their BMW, where they are going to find the world's perfect artichoke, and things like that.

NARRATOR: Sandy, if you were organizing and directing an oral history of the Reagan presidency, what are the questions that you would ask? What would you look for in terms of the essence of this presidency? What surprises lie there that you think one ought to probe? And how do you think history will judge this presidency?

MR. VANOCUR: Starting with the last question, and even taking into account these future revelations, I think history will treat Ronald Reagan pretty decently. I don't think he will be judged a near great President as I thought he would have been about a year ago. A lot depends on what he pulls off with the Soviet Union this summer. I think history will treat him rather decently for having done what Roosevelt did, which was to help us restore faith in ourselves.

He did something else that is remarkable. He detoxified the political bloodstream of this country. Since the death of John F. Kennedy, a very toxic, venomous strain had been introduced into the body politic of this country: the assassinations, the racial disturbances, the Vietnam War, and the drug culture. There was Watergate, and then the tragedy of the hostages in Iran for all those months, which was a terrible blow to the United States. You could not conduct the politics of civility in the United States.

The whole period harks back to the late 1940s when we "lost" China and suffered other setbacks. Ike restored a lot of our confidence in the 1950s. In 1980 along came Reagan, this really decent man, who would fulfill a similar purpose. I also have to give some credit to Tip O'Neill; together they detoxified the political system. Yet Reagan, more than anybody else, dampened the political rhetoric of this country and reduced the venom in our political bloodstream. We now can joke and talk about things we couldn't in the 1960s or the 1970s. I think that is Reagan's most remarkable achievement. I think it partly lies in the fact that he really is a *Saturday Evening Post* cover. He has this wonderful innocence about life, which I think is both one of the most endearing and yet troubling characteristics that runs through our politics, our diplomacy, and our literature. I think that somehow he was thrown up by political fortunes at the right time to give us back this sense of civility.

For example, he is a man absolutely without any rancor. Shortly after taking office, he heard that the Congress had struck a medal in honor of Robert Kennedy. Carter hated the Kennedys so much that he would never present it. Reagan heard about this and said that it was ridiculous, and he told Mike Deaver or someone else to get Mrs. Robert Kennedy and the family together and present the medal at the White House. I watched him coming back from South America. He left Brazil, and he went to Colombia. There President Betancourt delivered a really unconscionable speech, a terrible antigringo speech, but Reagan just absorbed it and made a very felicitous speech on our behalf. By the end of the day he had charmed the socks off this president. When Jesse Jackson brought Lieutenant Goodman to the White House and tried to upstage the President, there was Reagan, standing in the background, handling it just beautifully.

I'm at a stage now where I do believe that incense, emanations, and atmospherics are as important as substance to set a tone, because this marvelous country just lumbers along somehow. Perhaps that's the way to look at Ronald Reagan—not whether he was a good manager, nor whether his wife talked to an astrologer. (Looking at some of the advisers I've seen in my lifetime, an astrologer might have been as good!) He set a tone for the country, and we felt good about this man sitting in the White House. He is a remarkable president, and I think if you'd go at it from the point of view that he matches our American fantasy about ourselves you would have to like him. It is terribly important to have a better understanding of this man and what he has meant to America.

NARRATOR: I know all of you join me in thanking Sandy for returning to the University of Virginia. Thank you for being here.